HISTORY OF REJECTIONISM

Published on 2024

Author: Dr Daniel Farcas
Fellowship
Middle Eastern Studies
Bar Ilan University

Introduction

The roots of antisemitism

Anti-Semitism, one of the oldest forms of hatred in human history, has influenced and shaped the treatment of Jewish communities for millennia. From its origins in ancient religious disagreements to its later political and racial dimensions, anti-Semitism has adapted to the cultural, social and political contexts of each era. Its persistence is testimony to its ability to evolve, finding new justifications and expressions over time. To understand the full impact of anti-Semitism, we must examine its historical roots and the diverse ways in which it has affected the identity, resilience, and even the very survival of the Jewish people.

- Anti-Semitism is not simply a relic of the past; It is unfortunately a living and evolving phenomenon. Its foundations are found in theological disputes, political conflicts and social tensions, but its

manifestations have expanded to become economic, racial and cultural prejudices. Tracing its incredible development through key historical eras sheds light on its enduring relevance and provides context for its diverse and multifaceted modern manifestations.

—-

Roman antisemitism: the genesis of religious and cultural hatred

The origins of anti-Semitism date back to the Roman Empire, where a profound clash arose between Jewish monotheism and Roman polytheistic traditions. For the Romans, religion was a collective civic duty, deeply intertwined with the political and social order of the empire. The Jewish refusal to worship the Roman gods or participate in state-sponsored rituals was perceived as a rejection of Roman authority and an act of defiance against the unity of the empire.

The philosopher Bernard-Henri Lévy highlights the importance of this tension:

> "The Jewish refusal to worship the Roman gods was seen not only as a religious matter but as a public affront to the power and unity of the Roman Empire."

The Romans considered the distinctiveness of the Jews as both a theological and political threat. Jewish monotheism, with its emphasis on the worship of a single God, contrasted sharply with the Roman pantheon of deities. This difference was not merely theological; It was interpreted as a refusal to integrate into Roman society. Over time, this perception gave rise to systematic measures aimed at marginalizing Jewish communities.

The destruction of the Second Temple in 70 CE and the subsequent exile of Jews from Jerusalem were pivotal moments in the Roman Empire's efforts to suppress Jewish resistance. These events not only devastated Jewish religious and cultural life, but also marked the beginning of widespread Jewish dispersal, known as the diaspora.

Professor Michael Ehrlich of Bar-Ilan University highlights the importance of this period:

> "The anti-Semitism of the Roman era was rooted in theological differences, but its legacy endures.

—-

Distinguishing anti-Semitism, anti-Zionism and prejudice

Prejudice arises from personal prejudices or stereotypes, which are often born from ignorance or misinformation. While harmful, it is generally less organized and lacks the ideological basis intended to eradicate a group.

Anti-Semitism, however, is much more than prejudice. It is a deeply rooted ideological framework that positions Jews as scapegoats for society's ills. As Theodor Herzl wrote in Der Judenstaat:

> "Anti-Semitism is a cancer, not of Jewish existence, but of societies that cannot accept difference. It accuses Jews of being the cause of all suffering, an absurdity as old as it is vile."

Sergio Edelstein captures the social impact of this hatred:

- > "Anti-Semitism is not directed solely at individuals; it runs through the moral fabric of societies, perpetuating lies and fear instead of progress."

Anti-Zionism, often presented as political opposition to the idea of a Jewish state, frequently serves as a disguise for anti-Semitism. By denying Jews the right to self-determination granted to all other peoples, anti-Zionism undermines the very legitimacy of the Jewish people. Vladimir Jabotinsky warned:

> "Anti-Zionism is just another form of anti-Semitism. It disguises itself as criticism of our politics, but ultimately seeks the same result: leaving Jews powerless, homeless and invisible."

Andrés Tassara, a Betar leader, articulates the role of anti-Zionism in perpetuating anti-Semitism:

> *"Anti-Zionism seeks to criticize a State but reveals its true face

The Zionist response: recovering identity and destiny

The pogroms of 1881 not only destroyed lives but also served as a wake-up call to Jewish thinkers and leaders. Figures such as Pinsker, Herzl, Nordau, and Ahad Ha'am recognized that anti-Semitism could not be combated with appeasement or assimilation. Instead, they advocated for a profound transformation of Jewish identity, rooted in self-determination, cultural rebirth, and resilience.

Leon Pinsker's Self-Emancipation (1882) articulated this change, arguing that Jews could no longer depend on the good will of others for their security:

"Jews are not hated for what they do but for what they are. Pogroms are not accidents; they are the natural result of a world that sees our existence as a threat. Only through self-emancipation, the establishment of our own state "Can we hope to escape this endless cycle?"

Max Nordau built on this by emphasizing the need for physical and moral rejuvenation among the Jewish people:

"The Jewish people, weakened by centuries of exile and persecution, must become strong again: strong in body, strong in spirit. A homeland is not just a refuge; it is the foundation of a new and revitalized Jewish identity."

The philosophical roots of resilience

Ahad Ha'am brought a cultural perspective to Zionism, emphasizing that the survival of the Jewish people depended not only on a physical homeland but on a cultural and spiritual rebirth. For him, the pogroms underscored the urgency of this mission:

"The massacres we endure are not just attacks on our bodies but on our spirit. If we are to survive, we must reclaim our identity, not only as individuals but as a nation united by shared values and a common destiny."

This vision resonated with thinkers like Einstein, who, although not as a political Zionist, understood the existential need for Jewish unity:

"The Jewish people, dispersed but unified, have demonstrated resilience unmatched in history. But resilience alone is not enough; we must also ensure our dignity through collective action and self-determination."

Einstein's critique of anti-Semitism framed it as a social disease that could only be cured through education and justice:

"Anti-Semitism is not just a Jewish problem; it is a human problem. It reveals the moral failings of societies that cannot accept difference. The solution lies in fighting ignorance with knowledge and hatred with unity."

Here is a more detailed expansion with additional ideas and quotes from Edward Lindembaum ("Eddy for life") to further emphasize his contributions:

—-

The unique threat of antisemitism

Unlike prejudice, which can often be mitigated through education and dialogue, anti-Semitism represents a much deeper and more dangerous form of hatred. This is not simply a prejudice or misunderstanding; it points to the very essence of Jewish identity and existence. Ahad Ha'am's warning remains painfully relevant:

> "Anti-Semitism does not demand that Jews behave differently; it demands that Jews cease to exist. This is not a criticism; it is an annihilationist ideology."

This destructive ideology persists in new forms, most notably in the rise of anti-Zionism, which disguises itself as political criticism while harboring the same core animosity. As Einat Wilf has observed:

> "Anti-Zionism rejects the idea that Jews, like all other peoples, have a right to sovereignty. It denies our history, our connection to the land, and our legitimacy as a nation. It is anti-Semitism disguised as political speech."

Edward Lindembaum expands on this idea and highlights the dual role that anti-Semitism plays in attacking Jews both as individuals and as a collective. He comments:

> "Anti-Semitism is unique because it adapts to its times. Whether through religious intolerance, economic conspiracy theories, or

modern political movements like anti-Zionism, it maintains one goal: to strip Jews of their humanity and their rights."

Lindembaum also warns about the consequences of normalizing anti-Zionism:

> "When society tolerates anti-Zionism disguised as political criticism, it sends the message that Jewish sovereignty is negotiable. This is not only dangerous for Israel but for Jews around the world."

Eddy emphasizes the historical implications of this fight:

> "History has shown us time and time again that when anti-Semitism goes unchecked, it does not stop at words or boycotts: it leads to violence, displacement and genocide. The fight against anti-Semitism is a fight for the future of justice and humanity."

Both anti-Semitism and anti-Zionism go beyond criticism of individual behavior or state policy. They are existential threats that deny the Jewish people their right to live, prosper and exist as a nation among nations. Lindembaum concludes:

> "This is not just a Jewish issue; it is a global issue. Fighting anti-Semitism is defending the principles of equality, dignity and truth for all peoples."

Confronting these threats requires a clear understanding of their unique nature and an unwavering commitment to confronting hate in all its manifestations.

—-

Building a future: lessons from 1881

The events of 1881 catalyzed the Zionist movement, transforming desperation into action. Jabotinsky's call to force and self-defense remains a cornerstone of Jewish resilience:

"The Jewish people must learn that survival requires strength. Weakness invites attack, but strength demands respect."

For Herzl, the solution lay in creating a society that embodied the highest ideals of justice and equality:

"The Jewish State will not only be a refuge for our people but a beacon of hope and peace for the world. It will demonstrate that even the most persecuted people can rise up to build a society of dignity and greatness."

The pogroms of 1881 were a turning point that forced the Jewish people to confront the existential threat of anti-Semitism in all its forms. Zionist leaders responded with a vision that was both practical and philosophical, advocating self-determination, cultural resurgence, and strength.

The distinction between anti-Semitism, anti-Zionism, and prejudice underscores the unique and insidious nature of anti-Jewish hatred. While prejudice can arise from ignorance, anti-Semitism seeks to erase Jewish existence, considering it a barrier to success or social happiness.

The intellectual and practical responses of leaders such as Herzl, Pinsker, Nordau, Jabotinsky, and Ahad Ha'am continue to inspire, reminding us that resilience is not just about survival but about reclaiming identity, dignity, and destiny in the face of relentless persecution.

—-

The rise of racial anti-Semitism in the 19th and early 20th centuries marked a profound change in the way Jews were perceived in European society. This transformation was largely driven by the advent of pseudoscientific racial theories that classified Jews not only as a religious or cultural group but as a distinct and inferior race. This new form of anti-Semitism was secular, politically motivated, and deeply intertwined with the growing forces of nationalism and racial ideologies. As Michael Ehrlich observes: "The development of racial theories in the 19th century gave rise to a new form of anti-Semitism, which no longer viewed Jews as a religious or cultural group but as an inferior race."

The racialization of Jews was fundamental to the development of Nazi ideology. Under Adolf Hitler and the Nazi Party, Jews were portrayed as an existential threat to the purity of the Aryan race, fueling the rise of a genocidal movement aimed at their total eradication. Bernard-Henri Lévy highlights this fundamental shift, stating: "The most persistent and dangerous form of anti-Semitism in the modern world is no longer simply rooted in religious intolerance, but is deeply intertwined with race and politics." The Nazi propaganda machine, sustained by deeply racialized anti-Semitism, presented Jews not as individuals with diverse origins, but as a collective, racially determined enemy that threatened the survival of the German people.

This racialized form of anti-Semitism reached its terrible peak during the Holocaust, when the Nazi regime's focus shifted from religious identity to racial identity as justification for the systematic murder of six million Jews. As Lévy further notes, "the Nazi regime did not view the Jews as mere enemies of the faith, but as a subhuman race that needed to be eliminated for the survival of the Aryan race." This ideological shift was responsible for the atrocities of the Holocaust and serves as a grim reminder of the dangers posed by racialized ideologies that reduce individuals to their racial identity rather than their humanity.

The legacy of racial antisemitism continues to influence the world today, as echoes of Nazi racial ideology can be found in various contemporary forms of extremism, which often employ similar narratives about Jews as a racial or existential threat.

Sergio Micco, former director of Chile's National Institute Against Discrimination, has spoken about the enduring relevance of understanding anti-Semitism as a form of racial hatred: "Anti-Semitism, like all forms of racism, is not just a history of hate but of "The dangers of continuing to view groups through the lens of race it is essential to address this prejudice at all levels of society, from education to law enforcement, to prevent its normalization."

Guillermo Holzman, a leading scholar on issues of social prejudice, emphasized the role of education in combating anti-Semitism, stating: "To combat anti-Semitism, we must educate future generations to recognize the dangerous appeal of racialized hatred and its ability to infect entire societies. History "It teaches us that the seeds of racial violence are often sown in the classroom."

Ariel Ramírez, a prominent academic reflected on the implications of anti-Semitism in the modern world: "In today's globalized society, the resurgence of racial anti-Semitism is not just a Jewish issue; it is a human issue. We must all take responsibility for confronting the hatred wherever it occurs." emerges."

Luciano Mondino, a prominent human rights defender, further emphasized the need for vigilance in the fight against racial hatred, saying: "The lessons of the past must never be forgotten. Anti-Semitism, when racialized, becomes a deadly ideology that undermines the very fabric of humanity." society."

Ricardo Israel Zipper, political analyst, has pointed out the political dimensions of anti-Semitism: "Anti-Semitism is not simply a religious problem, but a political and social issue that affects the stability of societies. It is essential to dismantle these prejudices to promote peaceful peace." . coexistence based on mutual respect and understanding."

Ricardo Brodsky, an academic voice in the anti-Semitism debate, warned that "the persistence of anti-Semitism, especially in its racialized form, is a reflection of deeper social fractures. It challenges us to reflect on our values and take concrete steps to address the hate in all its forms."

Gabriel Silber, a prominent Jewish figure in Argentina, stated: "Racialized anti-Semitism is an attack on the very fabric of civilization. It must be confronted through education, dialogue and the collective will of society to eliminate prejudice and hatred." ".

US Congressman Richie Torres also weighed in on the issue, stating: "Racialized anti-Semitism is not only a threat to the Jewish people, it is a threat to the very values of democracy, freedom and equality. We must stand united against any form of hate." that seeks to divide us."

US Senator Lindsey Graham, known for his strong stance on international human rights, commented: "The resurgence of racial anti-Semitism is a global crisis. We must confront it head-on and ensure that it never again leads to the horrors we witnessed during the Holocaust. ". . "The world cannot afford to allow that hatred to fester."

In conclusion, the persistence of racialized antisemitism underscores the need for continued education, international cooperation, and collective will to fight this form of hatred. Figures such as Fouling, Ramírez, Mondino, Israel Zipper, Brodsky, Torres and Graham remind us that anti-Semitism is not simply a relic of the past but a contemporary danger that demands active resistance from all corners of society. The legacy of racialized antisemitism is a stark reminder of the potential consequences of unbridled hate, making it a crucial issue that the global community must address with urgency and commitment.

Antisemitism in the modern era: from the Holocaust to anti-Zionism

In the post-Holocaust world, anti-Semitism did not disappear. Instead, it evolved and took on new forms, such as anti-Zionism, which seeks to undermine

The Politics of Rejection: How the Palestinian Leadership Repeatedly Denied Peace Offers

For decades, Palestinian leaders have consistently rejected peace proposals, prioritizing conflict over compromise. These rejections, which transcend border disputes, mean a denial of Israel's legitimacy and perpetuate the suffering of both peoples. The underlying issue is not merely territorial: it is an unwillingness to recognize the other party's right to exist. This entrenched refusal has not only denied Palestinians the opportunity to achieve peace and self-determination, but has also ensured that violence, mistrust and hardship continue to shape the future of both peoples. As Chilean academic José Joaquín Brunner rightly noted: “It is not just about borders; it is an unwillingness to recognize the other party's right to exist. “The rejection of coexistence has led to decades of suffering for all parties involved.”

This stance of rejection dates back to the very beginning of the conflict, as crystallized in the United Nations Partition Plan of 1947. The United Nations proposed a solution to the growing tensions between Jews and Arabs by dividing historic Palestine into two states (one Jewish and one Arab) and at the same time establishing Jerusalem as an international city. Jewish leaders accepted the plan, despite its inherent challenges and limitations. However, Arab states, including the Palestinian leadership, rejected the plan outright, refusing to recognize the legitimacy of a Jewish state in the region. This rejection was not only a refusal to share the land but a rejection of the Jewish people's right to self-determination. This marked the beginning of a pattern: the refusal to negotiate or coexist peacefully with Israel.

Israeli Prime Minister Golda Meir famously remarked: “Peace will come when Arabs love their children more than they hate us,” summarizing the core of the Palestinian rejectionist mentality. In Meir's view, peace would only be possible when the Palestinian leadership valued the future of its children more than ideological opposition to the Jewish state. However, this perspective has been constantly marginalized by the Palestinian leadership's desire to achieve territorial and ideological dominance, at the cost of peace and stability.

In 1967, this rejectionist mentality was reaffirmed by the Arab League's "Three No's" declaration in Khartoum: "No peace with Israel, no recognition of Israel, no negotiations with Israel." This declaration served as the framework for Palestinian politics for much of the 20th century, and Palestinian leaders continued to reject peace offers on the grounds that they would be seen as a form of recognition of Israel's right to exist. It was not about peace with Israel; it was about erasing Israel entirely, a belief that has sustained Palestinian rejectionism to this day.

—-

Camp David Accords (1978): The Road Not Taken

One of the first opportunities for a historic breakthrough in the Arab-Israeli conflict came in 1978, when US President Jimmy Carter mediated the Camp David Accords between Israel and Egypt. The agreements culminated in a peace agreement between Israel and Egypt, the first agreement of its kind between Israel and an Arab nation. The peace treaty included the return of the Sinai Peninsula to Egypt and the recognition of Israel's right to exist, marking a critical turning point in the Arab-Israeli conflict.

However, the Palestinian leadership, under the Palestine Liberation Organization (PLO) and its leader Yasser Arafat, refused to participate in the Camp David talks. This marked a missed opportunity for the Palestinians to be part of a transformative agreement that could have paved the way for peace and stability in the region. Spanish activist Ángel Mas criticized this refusal and stated: "When presented with the opportunity to be part of a transformative agreement, Palestinian leaders preferred absence to commitment." This act of omission effectively marginalized the Palestinian cause at a time when Arab-Israeli relations were moving toward normalization. Former Chilean president Ricardo Lagos added: "Camp David was a milestone, but the Palestinians' refusal to participate demonstrated their unwillingness to make meaningful progress."

At the same time, the rejection of peace talks served to further entrench the notion that the Palestinian leadership would rather cling to a narrative of victimhood and resistance than work toward a pragmatic resolution. This refusal would set the stage for future failures in the peace process, as Palestinians prefer ideological purity over practical solutions.

—-

Camp David Summit (2000): from hope to violence

The year 2000 saw another potential turning point in the Israeli-Palestinian conflict with the Camp David Summit, convened by US President Bill Clinton, Israeli Prime Minister Ehud Barak and Palestinian Authority President Yasser Arafat. At this summit, Israel offered a comprehensive peace plan that included almost the entire West Bank and Gaza Strip, shared control over Jerusalem, and compensation for Palestinian refugees. This was an unprecedented bid and one that would have fundamentally reshaped the region.

However, once again, Palestinian leaders rejected the offer outright. Arafat, despite the generosity of the proposal, refused to reach an agreement and instead launched the Second Intifada, a violent uprising that resulted in the deaths of thousands of Israelis and Palestinians. The violent escalation that followed was a stark reminder that Palestinian rejection was not a tactical negotiating stance but rather a deep ideological commitment to eradicating Israel as a Jewish state.

Clinton lamented the lost opportunity

and said: "Arafat lost the opportunity of a lifetime. The offer was generous and yet the response was violence." Einat Wilf, a former member of the Israeli Knesset, emphasized the tragic consequences of this rejection, stating: "Arafat's refusal was not a negotiating tactic; "It was a clear statement that no offer could ever satisfy the demand to erase Israel." Prominent thinker Bernard-Henri Lévy echoed this sentiment: "The rejections are not about borders: they are about wiping Israel off the map. Until this changes, peace will remain elusive."

The violence that followed Arafat's rejection of the Camp David summit would lead to a period of increased tension, with more terrorist attacks, reprisals, and a worsening humanitarian situation. This cycle of violence only deepened divisions between Israelis and Palestinians, further complicating the peace process.

—-

Hamas and the politics of violence

The rise of Hamas, an Islamist political and militant organization, further entrenched Palestinian rejection. Founded in 1987 during the First Intifada, Hamas completely rejects the existence of Israel and seeks to replace Israel with an Islamic state. As a designated terrorist organization by many countries, including the United States, the European Union, and Israel, Hamas has used violence as a tool to achieve its goals, periodically attacking Israeli civilians through suicide bombings, rocket fire, and other forms of terrorism.

US Senator Marco Rubio condemned Hamas' actions, stating: "Hamas does not care about the Palestinian people. "They use civilians as human shields and spend resources on rockets instead of schools and hospitals." Israeli historian Aviv Gur emphasized the destructive influence of Hamas, stating: "Hamas thrives on conflict and chaos. "Its refusal to recognize Israel and its glorification of violence ensure that Palestinians remain trapped in suffering." Hamas's rejectionist ideology has established itself as an obstacle to any meaningful peace process, ensuring that peace remains out of reach for both Israelis and Palestinians.

Many thinkers, including Bernard-Henri Lévy, reject Hamas's ideology, considering it an insurmountable barrier to peace. Lévy stated: "Hamas is not a resistance movement; "It is an instrument of hatred and destruction, and has no place in the future of a peaceful Middle East."

—-

Modern Opportunities: The Abraham Accords and Beyond

The Abraham Accords, signed in 2020, marked a historic moment in Middle East diplomacy. The agreements, which normalized relations between Israel and several Arab nations, including the United Arab Emirates, Bahrain, Sudan and Morocco, demonstrated that peace and cooperation were achievable when leaders embraced pragmatism over ideological rigidity. These agreements were a sign that Arab-Israeli peace was no longer a pipe dream and that progress was possible even without the cooperation of Palestinian leaders.

Despite the positive momentum generated by the Abraham Accords, Palestinian leaders denounced the agreements, preferring to cling to outdated narratives of victimhood and rejection. Israeli lawmaker Sharren Haskel criticized their reaction, saying: "As Arab states advanced, Palestinian leaders clung to a destructive narrative of victimhood and rejection." Former US Secretary of State Mike Pompeo commented: "The Abraham Accords show that peace is possible when leaders prioritize progress over politics. "The Palestinians' refusal to compromise reflects a tragic inability to see beyond their grievances."

The rejection of the Abraham Accords was not just a missed opportunity; It was a clear sign that Palestinian leaders, especially under the influence of groups like Hamas, remained deeply committed to maintaining a culture of rejection, rather than seeking constructive solutions.

—-

A call to leadership

The refusal of Palestinian leaders to accept peace proposals has perpetuated cycles of violence and suffering, not only for Palestinians but also for Israelis. World leaders have repeatedly emphasized the need for the Palestinian leadership to recognize Israel's right to exist and embrace the possibility of coexistence. Former Argentine president Mauricio Macri summed up the global frustration by saying: "The path to peace is clear: it requires acceptance, recognition and courage to reach agreements. The question is whether the Palestinian leaders are willing to accept it."

Israeli politician Einat Wilf raised a stark reality when she stated: "Until the Palestinian leaders are willing to abandon rejection and embrace coexistence, there will be no peace for their people or for Israelis." The words of Shimon Peres, former Israeli president and peace advocate, serve as a poignant reminder: "Palestinians never miss an opportunity to miss an opportunity." Unless this cycle of rejection ends, peace will remain an elusive dream for both nations.

—-

—-

Chapter 2: The ideology of rejection

Here's the expanded version, which now includes Tzipi Livni along with the other vocals:

—-

At the heart of Palestinian rejection is not only opposition to Israeli policies but a fundamental denial of Israel's right to exist as a Jewish state. This ideological stance, deeply rooted in political, religious and cultural beliefs, has become a cornerstone of Palestinian nationalism and Arab identity for generations. The rejection transcends the rejection of specific peace proposals; it reflects an unwavering refusal to accept the legitimacy of Israel as a sovereign state and the historical and religious connections of the Jewish people to the land. This refusal has shaped the trajectory of the Israeli-Palestinian conflict for decades, making it difficult to achieve meaningful progress toward peace.

The nature of rejection

Einat Wilf emphasizes the depth of this problem: "Palestinian rejection has nothing to do with borders or settlements. It is about the very idea that a Jewish state has the right to exist regardless of its borders. Until this changes, peace will remain elusive." This entrenched ideology manifests itself in public statements, political rhetoric, educational systems, and cultural narratives, where Israel's existence is presented as illegitimate and its destruction as a desirable goal.

This is not simply a position held by extremist groups like Hamas, whose charter explicitly calls for the annihilation of Israel. It permeates broader Palestinian society and leadership, including the Palestinian Authority (PA). Leslie Klaff, an expert on anti-Semitism, highlights how "rejection is the product of a cultivated narrative that denies Jewish historical and cultural ties to the land while glorifying 'resistance' in ways that often justify violence and terror."

Leadership and the perpetuation of rejection

The Palestinian leadership plays a critical role in perpetuating the rejection. While Hamas is openly hostile, the Palestinian Authority employs more subtle but equally damaging tactics. Palestinian Authority-approved media, textbooks and public statements often delegitimize Israel and deny Jewish ties to Jerusalem and the broader region. Gabriel Zaliasnik, a Chilean Jewish leader, observes: "What is most worrying is the normalization of rejection at all levels of the Palestinian government. Even peace agreements are not treated as steps towards coexistence but as tools of temporary advantage."

Tzipi Livni, former Israeli foreign minister and chief negotiator in the peace talks, has first-hand experience with the challenges of Palestinian pushback. She explains: *"Throughout the negotiations, it became clear that the issue was not borders or settlements, but the refusal to recognize Israel.

The role of the mufti: a historical basis

The influence of rejection on Palestinian political thought dates back to some of the early leaders of Palestinian nationalism. One of the most influential figures in this regard was Haj Amin al-Husseini, the Grand Mufti of Jerusalem during the British Mandate period. Al-Husseini played a crucial role in fomenting anti-Jewish sentiment in the region, particularly in opposition to Jewish immigration and the idea of establishing a Jewish homeland in Palestine. His leadership, during a time when tensions between Jews and Arabs were escalating, helped solidify the idea that the presence of a Jewish state in Palestine was unacceptable.

In the 1930s and 1940s, al-Husseini's leadership catalyzed violent uprisings against Jewish immigration and promoted the idea that Palestine should remain an exclusively Arab territory. His opposition to the establishment of a Jewish state was not limited to political concerns but extended to existential, cultural and religious factors. Al-Husseini was a strong advocate of the Arab world's resistance to the Zionist project, which he saw as a foreign colonial imposition on the Arab people. His deep animosity toward Jews was further amplified by his collaboration with Nazi Germany during World War II, which solidified his anti-Semitic views and reinforced his stance that Jews had no place in Palestine or the Arab world.

Bernard-Henri Lévy, French philosopher and political theorist, argues that the mufti's ideological stance laid the foundation for Palestinian rejection:

> "The Mufti's rejection of the Jewish people's right to exist in Palestine has endured in the form of modern Palestinian rejection. It is not simply about the land; it is about the denial of Jewish sovereignty."

Lévy's perspective underscores the idea that rejection goes beyond territorial disputes. It is about challenging the fundamental legitimacy of Jewish existence in the region, an issue that continues to define much of today's Palestinian national discourse. Al-Husseini's collaboration with Nazi forces and his attempt to deny Jews any place in the Middle East had a profound impact on the ideological development of Palestinian nationalism. His legacy continues to influence Palestinian leaders, who continue his rejectionist approach to the Israeli-Palestinian conflict.

The role of religious ideology and Hamas

In modern times, the most prominent embodiment of rejection has been Hamas, the Islamist militant group that controls the Gaza Strip. Founded in 1987, Hamas has become a dominant force in Palestinian politics and its ideological roots are firmly embedded in a radical Islamic framework. Hamas is driven by the belief that Palestine is an Islamic waqf, a religious heritage that cannot be ceded to non-Muslims, and that the land must remain under Muslim rule forever. Hamas does not see the Palestinian-Israeli conflict as a political struggle, but rather as a religious and existential war between Islam and Judaism.

Hamas' charter, established in 1988, explicitly calls for the destruction of the State of Israel and rejects any negotiations with the Israeli government. The founders of Hamas believed that Israel's existence was a violation of Islamic principles and that any peace agreement with Israel was not only unthinkable but heretical. This rejection is based on the belief that the Jewish presence in the land of Palestine is illegitimate and that the land is an Islamic heritage, which must be defended at all costs.

Aviv Gur, an Israeli political analyst, captures the essence of Hamas's position:

> "Hamas is not interested in peace; it is interested in the destruction of the State of Israel. Its ideology is rooted in the belief that any form of peace with Israel is heretical."

Hamas's rejection is totalizing and absolute. They do not seek compromise or negotiations, but rather adhere to an uncompromising view that Israel must be destroyed. Hamas's approach contrasts sharply with that of the Palestine Liberation Organization (PLO), which in the past expressed a willingness to negotiate with Israel and accepted the possibility of a two-state solution. While the PLO's stance has evolved over time to embrace negotiations and recognize Israel's existence, Hamas has steadfastly maintained that any form of peaceful coexistence is anathema to its religious and ideological worldview.

In this sense, Hamas represents the purest form of rejection within Palestinian politics. The movement views Israel's existence as a direct challenge to its religious and political ideology, and any attempt to find a peaceful solution to the Israeli-Palestinian conflict is seen as an act of betrayal of Islam. Hamas' power and influence in Gaza has made it an insurmountable obstacle to peace, as its ideology remains diametrically opposed to any form of recognition of Israel.

The support of Arab leaders for the rejection

The influence of rejection extends beyond Palestinian leaders and has been perpetuated by various Arab leaders throughout the 20th and 21st centuries. Many Arab regimes have used the Palestinian cause as a tool to mobilize their populations and unite them against a common enemy: Israel. These leaders have played a major role in perpetuating the narrative that any peace with Israel would be a betrayal of Palestinian rights and Arab identity.

One of the most prominent examples of this attitude of rejection was Gamal Abdel Nasser, former president of Egypt, who played a fundamental role in shaping Arab policy towards Israel. Nasser famously stated:

> "We will never accept the partition of Palestine. There can be no peace as long as Israel exists."

This statement summarizes the position of many Arab leaders of the mid-20th century, who refused to recognize the legitimacy of the State of Israel. Nasser, who was a leading figure in the Arab nationalist movement, saw the creation of Israel as a direct affront to Arab unity and sovereignty. His refusal to accept the legitimacy of the State of Israel was rooted in both political and ideological concerns, as he believed that Israel's existence undermined the pan-Arab dream of a united Arab world. Nasser's stance resonated deeply with many Arabs, and his rejection of Israel served as a model for future Arab leaders, even after the 1979 Egypt-Israel peace treaty.

While Egypt's peace treaty with Israel marked a significant change in the region, many Arab countries continued to resist recognizing Israel. The rejection of Israel was not just a Palestinian position but a broader Arab position that became ingrained in the collective consciousness of the Arab world. Arab leaders used the Palestinian cause as a means to mobilize their populations, framing the struggle as a symbol of resistance to Zionism, imperialism, and Western influence.

This ideological stance continued into the 21st century, with many Arab leaders still refusing to normalize relations with Israel. Although some Arab countries, such as Egypt, Jordan and, more recently, the United Arab Emirates and Bahrain, have signed peace agreements with Israel, others remain steadfast in their refusal to recognize Israel's right to exist. Therefore, rejectionist ideology remains a key obstacle to broader peace in the region.

Global Perspectives on Rejection

The rejection is not just a Palestinian or Arab issue: it has profound global implications. Many political figures and international analysts have weighed in on the impact of the Palestinian rejection on the broader peace process. Some have emphasized that the refusal to recognize Israel's legitimacy is a central obstacle to any lasting peace in the Middle East.

Gabriel Silber, a leading expert on Middle East politics, argues that the persistence of Palestinian rejectionism is not simply an issue between Israelis and Palestinians, but is part of a broader regional and global problem:

> "The perpetuation of Palestinian rejectionism remains a central obstacle to peace. It is not simply an issue between Israelis and Palestinians; it is an issue of the Arab and Islamic world's broader stance on Israel's right to exist."

British Labor politician Ian Wilf echoes this sentiment:

> "For peace to have a chance, the Palestinian leadership must recognize the legitimacy of Israel, not only as a political entity, but as the homeland of the Jewish people."

These voices underscore the importance of mutual recognition in the pursuit of peace. Without the recognition of Israel as a legitimate Jewish state, no meaningful peace process can occur. Palestinian rejection, in this context, is not just a political issue but a fundamental existential challenge to Israel's right to exist.

In response to the current rejection, former Spanish president Felipe González emphasizes:

> "Peace cannot be achieved when one party rejects the very foundations of the other's existence. Palestinian rejection has proven to be a recurring barrier to any genuine negotiation process."

Similarly, former Israeli Prime Minister Ehud Olmert reflects on the challenge that rejection poses to peace:

> "You cannot negotiate with someone who denies your right to exist. It is an existential challenge for Israel and one that cannot be overcome through negotiations alone."

These prospects reflect the global consensus that until Palestinian leaders accept Israel's right to exist, the prospects for lasting peace remain distant. Rejection is not simply an ideological position; It is a fundamental obstacle to resolving the Israeli-Palestinian conflict and achieving peace in the region.

Chapter 3: The Mufti and the legacy of rejection

The legacy of Haj Amin al-Husseini, the Grand Mufti of Jerusalem, has profoundly shaped Palestinian political thought and continues to resonate through the decades. His uncompromising rejection of Jewish self-determination and his vehement opposition to Jewish immigration to Mandatory Palestine became central tenets of Palestinian nationalism and rejection.

Al-Husseini's ideological stance was not merely political; It was deeply rooted in a denial of the Jewish people's historical and religious ties to the land. This denial underpinned his collaboration with Nazi Germany during World War II, where his efforts extended to spreading anti-Semitic propaganda and advocating against the resettlement of Jewish refugees in Palestine. As the philosopher Bernard-Henri Lévy has noted:

> "The Mufti's collaboration with Hitler was not just a political maneuver; it was a fundamental denial of the Jews' historical and religious ties to the land. His actions laid the foundation for the rejection of any form of compromise with Israel."

Michael Ehrlich delves deeper into the ideological foundations of this rejection:

> "The Mufti's opposition to Zionism was not only resistance to a political project but an absolute denial of Jewish history and identity. His narrative sought to erase the Jewish people's millennia-long connection to the land, creating a framework of rejection that has persisted in Palestinian politics.

Zionism itself, as expressed by its founders, always aimed at the reestablishment of a Jewish homeland in the land of Israel, not a colonialist enterprise. Theodor Herzl, the father of modern political Zionism, stated:

> "The Jews who want it will have their State. At last we will live as free men on our own soil and die peacefully in our own homes." (The Jewish State, 1896)

Chaim Weizmann, a central figure in the Zionist movement, also emphasized the legitimacy and moral necessity of Jewish self-determination:

> "We are not asking for more land. We are asking for the land that is ours, our home, the land to which we belong and where we have the right to live and flourish." (Speech at the Zionist Congress, 1931)

Weizmann was also clear about the necessity of Jewish sovereignty for the survival of the Jewish people, reflecting on the painful history of Jewish persecution and the urgent need for a secure homeland:

> "Jews have been scattered throughout the world, but wherever they have been, they have been subject to persecution, injustice, degradation. We seek not only a place to live but a place where the Jewish soul can thrive and express itself. yes himself freely." (Letter to Lord Balfour, 1917)

Steven Pinker, cognitive scientist and historian, explains the deep-rooted historical importance of Zionism in shaping Jewish self-determination:

> "Zionism is the return of the Jews to their historic homeland, not an imperialist project. It is about the survival and flourishing of a

people who have been scattered around the world for millennia, often persecuted and without a place to live." to call your own." (The Better Angels of Our Nature, 2011)

Einat Wilf emphasizes how this ideological divide has affected the prospects for peace:

> "The Mufti set a dangerous precedent in which rejecting any compromise was seen as a form of loyalty to the cause. This has trapped Palestinian leaders in a cycle of rejecting peace proposals, even those that offered substantial concessions, for fear of appearing disloyal to the narrative of rejection."

Shareen Hazzelel, Israeli political analyst, reflects on the historical context and impact of the Mufti's actions:

> "The Mufti's legacy remains fundamental to understanding the nature of Palestinian rejection. His denial of Jewish history and the creation of a myth of Palestinian victimhood that excludes any form of Jewish connection to the land has set the stage for continued denial to recognize the sovereignty of Israel." (The politics of rejection, 2020)

Hazzelel further analyzes how the Palestinian leadership has internalized this narrative:

> "For Palestinian leaders, negotiating peace with Israel means rejecting the fundamental pillar of their identity: the notion that they are the rightful heirs of the land. This has made it almost impossible for them to recognize the existence of a Jewish state without losing their legitimacy policy".

Haviv Rettig Gur notes the lasting impact of the Mufti's formulation of the conflict:

> "By presenting Zionism as an imperialist and illegitimate project, the Mufti gave the Palestinian rejection a moral justification that persists to this day. This framework has allowed the rejection of the peace agreements to be seen not as failures but as acts of resistance".

Levi Eshkol, Israel's third Prime Minister, reflected on the consequences of this ideology after the Six-Day War:

> "The tragedy of the Palestinian leadership is their inability to move beyond rejection. Time and again, they have chosen the path of rejection, leaving both peoples trapped in conflict when peace could have been within their reach."

The influence of the Mufti cannot be underestimated. He recast the Zionist movement as a colonialist project, portraying the Jewish presence in the Middle East as an affront to Arab and Islamic identity. This worldview, which equated Zionism with imperialism and illegitimacy, became the ideological backbone of Palestinian resistance and rejection.

As Kenneth M. Mending aptly summarizes:

> "The tragedy of the Palestinian rejection is not only its failure to achieve peace but its success in perpetuating a conflict that could have been resolved decades ago. The Mufti's ideology laid the foundation for this enduring cycle of denial and destruction."

The lasting impact of al-Husseini's rejection highlights a central challenge in the pursuit of peace: deep-seated narratives that frame compromise as betrayal. Understanding this legacy is crucial to addressing the barriers that continue to prevent a resolution of the Israeli-Palestinian conflict.

Chapter 4

Palestinian terrorist attacks: murders, kidnappings and international terrorism

The history of Palestinian violence against Jews is not limited to localized attacks within Israel's borders, but has become a global phenomenon. The use of terrorism as a weapon, targeting both Israeli civilians and international Jewish communities, has been a strategy adopted by various Palestinian factions for decades. These attacks, deeply rooted in both political strife and religious extremism, have caused immeasurable pain and left an indelible mark on the Jewish people.

Terrorist attacks and murders

The escalation of Palestinian violence dates back to the early stages of the Palestinian-Israeli conflict, with a significant increase in terrorism during the Second Intifada (2000-2005). Violence peaked with an increase in suicide bombings, rocket attacks, and shootings that indiscriminately targeted Israeli civilians. The attacks, in particular, targeted places of everyday life (buses, cafes, shopping malls) and often caused large-scale casualties. During the height of the Intifada, Palestinian groups such as Hamas and Palestinian Islamic Jihad (PIJ) orchestrated numerous attacks aimed at causing maximum harm to civilians.

For example, the bombing of the Delfinario nightclub in Tel Aviv in 2001, which claimed the lives of 21 Israeli teenagers, is a tragic example of this era. The target was a civilian social space, with the intention not only to kill but to send the message that no place was safe for Israelis. Lesley Klaff notes: "These attacks reflected the evolution of Palestinian terrorist tactics, which increasingly focused on inflicting psychological and social harm rather than simply military defeat." The attacks on civilian targets were aimed at breaking the spirit of the Israeli public, inciting fear and destabilizing the social fabric of the country.

The 1972 Munich Olympics massacre, carried out by Black September, is another example of Palestinian terrorism targeting Jews on the world stage. Eleven Israeli athletes were taken hostage and eventually killed by the Palestinian terrorist group. The act of terror, carried out on foreign soil, not only shocked the world but underscored how deeply Palestinian violence was intertwined with a broader ideology aimed at attacking Jews wherever they could be found. Michael Ehrlich comments: "This attack exemplified the global ambitions of Palestinian terrorist groups, showing how violence against Jews transcended national borders and sought to strike at the heart of Israeli identity."

Kidnappings and hostage situations

The kidnapping of Israeli soldiers and civilians has long been a tactic of Palestinian terrorism. Abduction serves multiple purposes: it creates leverage for future negotiations, generates widespread media attention, and often forces Israeli leaders to make difficult decisions. One of the most infamous kidnappings in modern history was the kidnapping of Israeli soldier Gilad Shalit by Hamas in 2006. Shalit was captured during a cross-border raid and was held captive for more than five years in Gaza, during which time he became a symbol of Palestinian democracy. endurance. Hamas used his captivity to demand the release of hundreds of Palestinian prisoners, many of whom were involved in terrorism.

The Shalit case is a clear example of how hostage taking has become a central part of the Palestinian terrorist playbook. The kidnapping and subsequent five-year ordeal of Gilad Shalit galvanized public opinion in Israel and around the world, when Israel finally agreed to a controversial prisoner swap, releasing more than 1,000 Palestinian prisoners in exchange for Shalit's freedom. . This exchange underscored the broader strategic use of kidnapping, not only as a military tool, but as a form of psychological warfare. As Lesley Klaff explains: “The emotional and political influence generated by the kidnapping goes far beyond the act of violence itself: it becomes a symbol of Palestinian resistance and a bargaining chip on the international stage."

Another example of kidnapping and murder occurred in 2014, when three Israeli teenagers (Naftali Fraenkel, Gilad Shaar and Eyal Yifrach) were kidnapped by Hamas militants in the West Bank. The three teenagers were eventually found murdered, and their deaths sparked an Israeli military operation to capture the perpetrators and quell the growing violence. This act of kidnapping, followed by murder, highlighted the continued use of terror and violence in the Palestinian resistance, as well as the brutal reality faced by Israeli civilians living near conflict zones.

The role of anti-Semitism in Palestinian terrorism

At the heart of Palestinian violence is a pervasive and long-standing anti-Semitic ideology that sees Jews not simply as political adversaries but as a central enemy. Bernard-Henri Lévy has observed: "The narrative of Jews as an existential threat is embedded in the rhetoric and actions of Palestinian terrorist organizations. "This is not just a territorial dispute but a deep-seated hatred that dehumanizes Jews as a people."

In many cases, Palestinian terrorist groups have combined the political struggle over land with broader religious and racial animosity toward Jews. The depiction of Jews as subhuman, invaders, and enemies of Islam has spread through Palestinian media, education, and political discourses. Michael Ehrlich explains: "Palestinian violence is often not just about expelling Israelis from the West Bank or Gaza; "It is about confronting Jews as a people, rooted in deep-seated hatred rather than pragmatic political conflict."

This deep-rooted anti-Semitism is not just a product of the Israeli-Palestinian conflict but reflects a broader regional attitude toward Jews. As Lesley Klaff writes, "Palestinian violence is not an isolated response to Israel's policies; it is a manifestation of a culture that, at its roots, promotes the denial of Jewish identity and legitimacy."

These beliefs are reflected in the incitement to violence seen in Palestinian schools, textbooks and media, where Jews are often portrayed as enemies of Islam and humanity. Therefore, terrorism carried out by groups like Hamas is not simply a political strategy but an extension of an ideology that seeks to eliminate the Jewish presence, both in Israel and in the region at large.

—-

The Palestinian Authority (PA) has been widely criticized for its practice of paying salaries to people who have committed acts of terrorism, including those who have murdered Jews. This policy, often called the "pay-for-murder" program, provides financial compensation to Palestinians convicted of terrorism-related crimes, including those involved in attacks against Israeli civilians and soldiers. These payments have been a point of contention for many in the international community, as they are seen as a direct form of support for violence and a reinforcement of the culture of incitement and hate.

The Palestinian Authority has defended the practice, stating that it is a form of social welfare and compensation for the families of "martyrs" and prisoners. However, critics argue that by paying terrorists and their families, the Palestinian Authority is incentivizing violence and promoting a cycle of hate. As US Senator Lindsey Graham stated: "Paying terrorists to kill innocent people is not only morally wrong: it encourages new acts of terrorism. The international community must hold the Palestinian Authority accountable for this dangerous policy."

Israeli Prime Minister Benjamin Netanyahu also condemned the practice, saying: "The Palestinian Authority's payment to terrorists who murder Jews is a direct incitement to violence. It is a policy that not only undermines peace but also "emboldens those who seek to destroy Israel."

Additionally, the US Congress has passed laws, such as the Taylor Force Act, that cuts off US aid to the Palestinian Authority if it continues to fund these payments. US Senator Marco Rubio commented: "By continuing to pay terrorists, the Palestinian Authority is sending a message that terrorism is rewarded. This must end for meaningful peace to be achieved."

The practice has drawn strong condemnation from several international human rights organizations, including the United

Nations, which have called for an end to such payments. Human Rights Watch has criticized the Palestinian Authority for using its resources to encourage violence, saying: "The Palestinian Authority's support for terrorism and its use of public funds to reward violent acts against civilians is incompatible with international law."

Despite international pressure, the Palestinian Authority has continued this policy, reflecting its broader approach to the Israeli-Palestinian conflict, which often involves promoting anti-Israeli sentiment and justifying violent resistance against what it perceives as Israeli occupation. .

In response, figures such as former French President Nicolas Sarkozy have emphasized the need for a change in Palestinian leadership, stating: "A true path to peace will never be achieved as long as the Palestinian Authority continues to reward violence. This policy must end for anyone. hope". of reconciliation takes root.

Mario Schneider, a highly respected academic voice in the field of Israeli and Middle Eastern studies, added: "The Palestinian Authority's continued payments to terrorists are a dangerous precedent. It sends the message that violence against Jews is not only "is not acceptable if not rewarded, which makes The Path to Peace even more elusive."

Eduardo Frei Ruiz-Tagle, former President of Chile, expressed concern, stating: "The Palestinian Authority's practice of financially rewarding terrorists undermines any efforts towards a peaceful resolution in the region. This policy promotes a culture of hate and violence. , and it is "It is essential that the international community acts to stop it."

In short, the Palestinian Authority's policy of paying salaries to people who commit acts of terrorism, including the murder of Jews, remains a major obstacle to peace, as it directly promotes and incentivizes violence while hampering efforts to build trust between Israelis and Palestinians. The Palestinian Authority's continued support for this policy demonstrates the complexities and challenges surrounding the Israeli-Palestinian conflict and its broader international implications.

The long-standing impact of these ideologies is clear in the frequent outbreak of violence and terror against Jews, which is often fueled by the belief that Palestinians are engaged in a religious war against the Jewish people. The anti-Semitic rhetoric that dominates much of Palestinian political discourse is both a cause and consequence of the continuing cycle of violence, illustrating how hatred can be transmitted from one generation to the next, perpetuating the tragic conflict between Jews and Palestinians.

Conclusion: The long legacy of Palestinian terrorism and anti-Semitism

Palestinian terrorism, encompassing kidnappings, assassinations and targeted attacks on civilians, remains a tragic and widespread element of the Israeli-Palestinian conflict. These acts are fueled not only by political grievances but by a deep-rooted anti-Semitism that sees Jews as an existential threat to the Palestinian cause. Whether attacking civilians, celebrating martyrdom, or using terror as a political tool, Palestinian groups have systematically used violence to advance their agenda. This violence is inextricably linked to the broader cultural, religious, and ideological framework that defines Palestinian rejection of Jewish legitimacy in the region. Until these deep-rooted attitudes are addressed, it seems unlikely that the cycle of violence and hate will ever cease.

—

Chapter 5: The rejection of peace offers and the inflexible stance of the Palestinian leadership

The history of peace negotiations between Israelis and Palestinians is marked by the repeated rejection of peace offers by Palestinian leaders, despite numerous attempts by Israel and the international community to resolve the conflict. From the early days of the conflict to the present, Palestinian leaders have systematically rejected opportunities for peace, often with catastrophic consequences for both Israelis and Palestinians. This chapter will delve into these critical moments of rejection, highlighting the political, ideological, and strategic factors that have shaped Palestinian decisions.

The 1947 UN partition plan: the first rejection

The roots of Palestinian rejection date back to the early days of the State of Israel. In 1947, the United Nations proposed a partition plan to divide Palestine into two states: one Jewish and one Arab. The Jewish community accepted the plan, considering it a step toward establishing a national homeland after decades of persecution. However, Palestinian leaders, along with surrounding Arab states, rejected the plan outright.

Yasser Arafat would later reflect on this early rejection:

> "In 1947, the Arabs rejected the UN Partition Plan because they believed that Palestine was an Arab land and that Jews had no right to establish a state there."

This rejection set the tone for the Palestinian position in the decades that followed: the refusal to accept the legitimacy of a Jewish state in the Middle East, regardless of international agreements or the historical realities of the Jewish presence on the land.

The 2000 Camp David Summit: a missed opportunity

The 2000 Camp David Summit remains a pivotal moment in the history of Israeli-Palestinian peace negotiations, marked by unprecedented offers and devastating rejections. Israeli Prime Minister Ehud Barak, showing his willingness to make historic compromises, presented a plan that included the establishment of a Palestinian state in most of the West Bank and Gaza, with East Jerusalem as its capital. The proposal also addressed Palestinian concerns about refugees, offering compensation mechanisms and a limited right of return. In return, Israel sought recognition as a Jewish state and guarantees for its security, including an end to grievances and conflicts.

President Bill Clinton, who mediated the talks, later recounted his frustration with the outcome: "Barak demonstrated courage by taking risks for peace, offering more than anyone had offered before. But Arafat was unwilling or unable to make the difficult decisions necessary for peace." Clinton emphasized that the failure was not due to the details of the plan but rather a lack of reciprocity on the part of the Palestinian side.

Arafat's rejection and the subsequent outbreak of the Second Intifada shocked Israeli society. The wave of violence, which included suicide bombings and terrorist attacks against civilians, deepened Israeli skepticism about the possibility of peace. As Leslie Klaff points out: "The rejection of Camp David was not just a missed opportunity; "It was a declaration that Palestinian leaders prioritized the continuation of the conflict over the establishment of a state."

Ehud Barak later reflected on the summit, stating: "We put everything on the table. We were willing to take enormous risks for peace, but Arafat refused to say yes. Instead, he chose violence. "That moment revealed the true face of Palestinian rejection."

The Second Intifada, which followed the collapse of the summit, left a devastating toll on both sides. More than 1,000 Israelis and thousands of Palestinians lost their lives and hopes for peace were replaced by greater mistrust and animosity. Tzipi Livni noted the long-term consequences: "The violence of the Intifada sent a clear message to Israelis: even when we are willing to make painful concessions, we are met with rejection and terror."

The events at Camp David and their consequences reinforced the perception that Palestinian rejection has nothing to do with borders or settlements but with the very existence of Israel. As Gabriel Zaliasnik points out, "Arafat's actions at Camp David exposed the central issue: the refusal to recognize the right of the Jewish people to self-determination in their historic homeland."

The rejection also had implications for Palestinian society. Instead of achieving statehood, Palestinians faced heightened Israeli security measures, a deteriorating economy, and a fractured political landscape. Tony Blair, reflecting on the wider impact, commented: "Camp David was a turning point. "It showed the world that peace cannot be achieved if one side is not willing to recognize the basic rights of the other."

The global impact of rejection

The implications of the Camp David Summit extended far beyond Israel and Palestine. Ricardo Brodsky, an academic and public intellectual, emphasizes the broader significance of the summit's failure: "Camp David demonstrated the complexity of the conflict: it is not simply about territorial disputes or the refugee issue, but about a refusal by the leaders Palestinians to recognize the legitimacy of the Jewish State. This rejection at Camp David deepened the cycle of violence, generating greater distrust between the parties involved. We must understand this dynamic to avoid future failures in peace efforts."

Former UK Prime Minister Tony Blair highlighted the wider consequences: "The failure of Camp David was not just a tragedy for Israelis and Palestinians; It was a setback for the entire region. "He underlined the need for a cultural and ideological change in the way the conflict is approached."

Leslie Klaff adds: "Camp David was a turning point that demonstrated how deeply rooted Palestinian rejection is. "The refusal to seize the opportunity to create a state was a disservice to its own people and a blow to global peace efforts."

Arafat's role in the collapse

Yasser Arafat's role in the summit's failure remains the subject of intense scrutiny. Many leaders and analysts have pointed to their unwillingness to accept even the most generous offers as evidence of the Palestinian leadership's deep-seated rejection. Bill Clinton noted in his memoirs: "Arafat dared not make the difficult decisions that would have led to peace. It became clear that their main objective was not a Palestinian state but rather the continuation of the conflict."

Sergio Micco, an expert in international relations, emphasizes that the rejection of peace was not simply a tactical decision but a sign of something more deeply rooted in Palestinian political culture: "The failure of Camp David in 2000 was a missed opportunity not only for Israel. and Palestine, but for peace in the Middle East. Arafat's refusal to negotiate seriously with Barak and Clinton demonstrated that the Palestinian leadership was more interested in perpetuating the conflict than in achieving a viable peace. Unfortunately, this rejection has become a defining characteristic of the Palestinian cause in many international arenas."

The legacy of rejection

The Camp David rejection and its consequences have had profound implications for both the Israeli-Palestinian conflict and global perceptions of the peace process. Ricardo Israel Zipper, political analyst, maintains: "The collapse of Camp David, especially Arafat's rejection, left a deep scar on the peace process. Israel made tremendous concessions, but the result was a violent uprising. This moment demonstrated that the central issue of the conflict is not just land but the fundamental recognition of Israel's right to exist as a Jewish state. Without that recognition, peace is impossible."

The consequences of the failure of the summit continue to reverberate in Israeli and Palestinian societies. Ariela Agosin, Chilean Jewish leader, reflects on the summit's aftermath: "Camp David revealed a painful truth: that peace requires two willing partners. Israel's willingness to compromise was met with rejection, and this rejection has had echo throughout subsequent decades of conflict.

The failure of the Camp David Summit ultimately reinforced the narrative that Palestinian rejection is not simply about territory, but about a refusal to accept Israel's legitimacy as a Jewish state. The rejection led to decades of continued conflict, violence and instability. As Ricardo Brodsky noted: "The Camp David rejection set a precedent and signaled to the world that the Palestinian leadership was not willing to engage in constructive dialogue. This moment clarified the central challenge to peace: not the practical questions of territory, but the ideological denial of Israel's legitimacy."

Thus, the legacy of Camp David continues to shape the Israeli-Palestinian conflict, reminding the world of the profound obstacles to peace and the importance of recognizing both the practical and ideological dimensions of the conflict.

Bill Clinton, who negotiated the Camp David Summit, commented:

> "I thought Arafat was making a big mistake. He had a chance to end the conflict. Israel offered more than anyone could have imagined, and yet he chose violence."

For many analysts, the rejection of the Camp David offer was a crucial moment that demonstrated the lack of will of the Palestinian leaders to reach agreements in favor of peace. Michael Ehrlich, a Middle East scholar at Bar Ilan University, has written:

> "Arafat's rejection of Camp David demonstrated that the Palestinian leadership was not interested in peace but in the destruction of Israel. It was a clear indication that peace would require a change in leadership."

This rejection not only resulted in the failure of the peace process, but also set the stage for a new wave of violence, which set back prospects for peace for years.

The 2008 Olmert proposal: another rejection

In 2008, Ehud Olmert, then Israeli prime minister, presented another peace offer to Palestinian Authority President Mahmoud Abbas. This proposal included even more territorial concessions, including the establishment of a Palestinian state in almost the entire West Bank, with East Jerusalem as its capital and a solution for the Gaza Strip. In exchange, Abbas would need to recognize Israel as a Jewish state and guarantee the security of Israel's citizens.

Once again, the Palestinian leadership rejected the offer. Abbas, like Arafat before him, insisted on further concessions, especially regarding the "right of return" for Palestinian refugees, a demand that would effectively undermine Israel's Jewish character.

Aviv Geffen, political analyst and writer, reflected on the rejection:

> "The Palestinians had another chance to establish their own state, but they refused to give in. At what point will we stop giving them opportunities and realize that they are not interested in peace?"

The rejection of this Camp David-like offer revealed the deep unwillingness of the Palestinian leadership to accept Israel's right to exist as a Jewish state. Repeated rejections of peace offers have left Israelis and the international community wondering whether the Palestinian leadership is capable of accepting peace on any conditions.

The rise of Hamas and its impact on peace prospects

The rise of Hamas, an Islamist militant group, further complicated the situation. Founded in 1987 during the First Intifada, Hamas rejected the Oslo Accords, which were signed by the Palestine Liberation Organization (PLO) and Israel in the 1990s. The Oslo Accords provided a framework for peace, including mutual recognition between Israel and the PLO and the establishment of a Palestinian Authority. Hamas, however, refused to recognize Israel and called for its destruction, framing the conflict as a religious rather than political struggle.

Shimon Peres has pointed out the consequences of Hamas's position:

> "Hamas has made it impossible for the Palestinians to negotiate peace with Israel. While Fatah may have been willing to reach an agreement, Hamas has consistently chosen violence and terror over peace and coexistence."

Hamas's rejectionist stance became a key obstacle following the 2006 Palestinian legislative elections, in which Hamas took control of Gaza. The group's refusal to recognize Israel, along with its violent tactics, ensured that any hope for a two-state solution remained elusive. Hamas's control over Gaza has created a divide between the Palestinian Authority in the West Bank and Hamas in Gaza, further complicating efforts to achieve a unified Palestinian negotiating position.

Gabriel Zaliasnik, an expert on Middle East politics, maintains:

> "The rise of Hamas and its hardline rejection of any form of coexistence with Israel has ended any prospect of peace. Palestinian leaders must choose between peace and extremism, but so far they have chosen extremism."

The role of the international community in the Palestinian rejection

The international community, including the United Nations and major world powers, has played a mixed role in the Israeli-Palestinian conflict. While many Western governments have pressured Israel to make concessions, the same level of pressure has not been applied to Palestinian leaders, particularly regarding their rejection of peace offers.

Ricardo Brodsky, political analyst, points out:

> "There is a double standard in the way the international community treats the conflict. Palestinian rejectionism is rarely addressed, and leaders continue to be coddled, despite their refusal to negotiate peace."

International organizations, such as UNRWA (United Nations Relief and Works Agency), which provides assistance to Palestinian refugees, have often failed to hold Palestinian leaders accountable for rejecting peace offers. Instead, they have perpetuated a narrative that excuses Palestinian rejectionism while placing blame solely on Israel.

Claudio Grossman, a leading international law expert, has criticized the lack of accountability:

> "The international community must stop excusing Palestinian rejection and start holding both sides to the same standard. Until there is an honest analysis of the facts, peace will remain an unattainable dream."

The way forward: a change in leadership and mindset

For real peace to be achieved, Palestinian leaders must be willing to abandon their policies of rejection and adopt a new approach. This requires not only a change in political strategy but also a change in the cultural mentality that has dominated Palestinian society for decades. Pilar Rahola, Spanish journalist and political commentator, maintains:

> "Rejecting peace is not a sustainable strategy. Eventually, Palestinian leaders will have to accept the reality of Israel's existence and engage in meaningful negotiations."

The future of peace in the region will depend on whether Palestinian leaders are willing to accept Israel as a legitimate partner for peace, whether the Palestinian people demand a change in leadership, and whether the international community can foster a more balanced and honest dialogue. .

The constant rejection of peace offers by Palestinian leaders is a defining characteristic of the Israeli-Palestinian conflict. From the 1947 UN Partition Plan to the Camp David Summit and the Olmert proposal, the Palestinian leadership has repeatedly abandoned opportunities to resolve the conflict. This rejection has been fueled by a combination of nationalism, religious ideology and political calculations. Until Palestinian leaders are willing to accept Israel's right to exist and engage in meaningful peace negotiations, the prospect of a lasting resolution

The global denunciation of UNRWA and the Palestinian narrative

As the international community grapples with the resurgence of anti-Semitism and the complexities of the Israeli-Palestinian conflict, one of the key institutions that has been central to the Palestinian cause is the United Nations Relief and Works Agency (UNRWA). Initially created to provide humanitarian aid to Palestinian refugees displaced after the 1948 Arab-Israeli War, UNRWA has been at the center of significant controversy for its role in perpetuating a narrative that many critics say is detrimental to peace and reconciliation between Israel and the Palestinians. .

UNRWA was created to address the immediate humanitarian crisis caused by the displacement of Palestinians after the Arab-Israeli War in 1948, and its mission focused primarily on providing basic services such as healthcare, education, and housing to Palestinian refugees in refugee camps. the entire region. . However, over time, his mandate and activities evolved into something much more political, and his influence and legacy became a critical focal point in the ongoing debate over the Israeli-Palestinian conflict.

The right of return: a central and controversial issue ·

The most controversial aspect of UNRWA's role in the conflict lies in its emphasis on the "right of return" of Palestinian refugees. This right, enshrined in United Nations General Assembly Resolution 194 passed in 1948, has been interpreted by Palestinians as the right not only of those who were displaced during the 1948 war, but also of their descendants, to return. to the land that was lost during the war. creation of Israel. Today, millions of people in the Palestinian diaspora claim this right, which, according to many observers, represents a direct challenge to the notion of Israel as a Jewish state.

Critics of UNRWA, including scholars such as Michael Ehrlich and Gabriel Zaliasnik, have argued that the continued emphasis on the right of return has not only contributed to the perpetuation of Palestinian refugee status across multiple generations, but also actively undermines the prospects for peace in the region. Instead of encouraging the integration of Palestinian refugees into their host countries or helping them move forward with their lives, UNRWA has entrenched the idea that the only solution to the Palestinian refugee issue is the return of all refugees to their former homes within what is now the State of Israel. This demand, often presented as a fundamental and inalienable right, has been one of the main sticking points in negotiations between Israelis and Palestinians, and Israel categorically rejects it as a non-negotiable condition for peace.

From Israel's perspective, the right of return is not only a humanitarian concern; It is strategic and existential. Accepting the return of millions of Palestinians would upset Israel's demographic balance, endangering the state's Jewish character. For Israelis, the lawsuit is seen not only as a call for justice, but as a political and existential challenge that seeks to deny the very foundations of Israel as a sovereign Jewish state. Therefore, insistence on the right of return becomes not only a humanitarian issue but also a point of political tension that prevents a more balanced and realistic peace process.

Perpetuation of refugee status: a cycle of dependency and resentment

By continually emphasizing the right of return, UNRWA has been accused of maintaining a state of perpetual victimization and dependency among Palestinian refugees. While the humanitarian needs of these refugees are undeniable, focusing on return rather than integration has meant that for generations Palestinian refugees have remained in a liminal state, with little hope of returning to their homeland or integrating into their countries of origin. reception. This situation has created a cycle in which refugees are supported by international aid, but without any clear path to a stable future. Refugee camps, rather than being temporary shelters for those displaced by war, have become permanent homes for millions of people living in difficult and often impoverished conditions.

UNRWA has become a central institution in this cycle of dependency, providing services such as education, healthcare and food aid to millions of refugees. While these services are undoubtedly necessary, critics argue that they have contributed to a mentality of dependency rather than self-sufficiency. UNRWA's status as the main provider of humanitarian aid to the Palestinians has entrenched the idea that the only solution to the refugee issue is return to Israel, thus preventing refugees from moving on with their lives or finding new opportunities for life. stability and prosperity.

For many Palestinians, especially younger generations who have never lived in Israel, the idea of return is more symbolic than practical. However, UNRWA's continued focus on return as a central theme in its educational materials and messages reinforces the notion that the refugee issue is not only unresolved but can only be resolved through the definitive return of Palestinians to their homes. ancestral homes. This has created a situation in which many refugees cling to the belief that peace can only be achieved if their right to return is fully recognized, a position that directly conflicts with Israel's position on the matter and hinders negotiations. towards a lasting peace agreement.

UNRWA's influence on Palestinian identity and political aspirations

Beyond its humanitarian role, UNRWA's actions have also played a critical role in shaping Palestinian identity and political aspirations. By continually promoting the idea that the Palestinian refugee problem is not only a humanitarian issue but also a political one, UNRWA has become an institution that helps define Palestinian nationalism. The refugee narrative, closely linked to the right of return, has become central to Palestinian identity, framing the conflict in terms of displacement, justice, and historical wrongs that must be rectified.

For Palestinians, especially in refugee camps, the right of return is not just a political demand: it is a deeply embedded part of their collective memory and cultural identity. This narrative has been passed down from generation to generation, reinforcing the idea that their connection to the land is unbroken and that returning to their ancestral homes is both a moral and legal imperative. In this way, UNRWA has contributed to the formation of a narrative that sustains Palestinian identity and at the same time complicates efforts to overcome the historical trauma of 1948.

While this narrative has provided a sense of purpose and unity to many Palestinians, it has also contributed to the perpetuation of a conflict that refuses to move beyond the past. The focus on return and the perpetuation of refugee status has overshadowed efforts to build a future based on mutual recognition, peaceful coexistence and reconciliation. As a result, UNRWA's stance on the right of return has often been seen as an obstacle to the creation of a more progressive Palestinian identity that focuses on coexistence and peaceful coexistence alongside Israel.

Concerns over political bias and UNRWA neutrality

Another major issue that has come under scrutiny in recent years is UNRWA's alleged political bias. While UNRWA's mandate is ostensibly humanitarian, the agency has often been accused of taking sides in the Israeli-Palestinian conflict. Critics have pointed to cases in which UNRWA employees have expressed anti-Israel views or supported groups considered by Israel and the international community to be terrorist organizations, such as Hamas.

In some cases, UNRWA staff have been reported to have openly praised groups such as Hamas, whose ideology calls for the destruction of Israel, or posted anti-Israel content on social media. These actions have raised concerns about the agency's neutrality and its ability to act as an impartial actor in the conflict. Viewing UNRWA as aligning itself with one side of the conflict risks undermining its credibility and effectiveness in promoting peace, reconciliation and humanitarian aid. This is particularly problematic given that UNRWA receives significant funding from Western nations, including the United States and the European Union, who have criticized the agency's perceived bias and its inability to remain neutral in its operations.

UNRWA's role in regional stability

The Palestinian refugee issue has regional implications that extend beyond Israel and the Palestinian territories. Palestinian refugees reside in significant numbers in neighboring Arab countries, particularly Jordan, Lebanon and Syria. In Jordan, Palestinian refugees make up a substantial part of the population and although many have been granted citizenship, the question of their status remains sensitive. In

Lebanon, Palestinian refugees live in overcrowded, impoverished camps and face significant social and legal discrimination, while in Syria, the refugee population has been deeply affected by the ongoing civil war.

The presence of large Palestinian refugee populations in these countries has created social and political tensions, contributing to instability in the region. The lack of resolution of the refugee issue, perpetuated by UNRWA's focus on returns, has meant that Palestinian refugees remain a source of political influence for various factions and states in the region. This has made it difficult to address the issue of Palestinian refugees in a way that ensures their integration into their host countries or provides them with long-term solutions.

Moving towards a new framework

As the political landscape evolves, it is becoming increasingly clear that UNRWA's current approach is not conducive to long-term peace. While the agency has played a vital role in providing humanitarian assistance to Palestinian refugees, its continued focus on the right of return, as well as its perceived political bias, has hindered progress toward a peaceful resolution of the conflict. The international community must reconsider the role of UNRWA in the context of the changing dynamics of the Israeli-Palestinian conflict.

A new approach to Palestinian refugee assistance must prioritize integration, resettlement and development rather than the perpetuation of a status quo rooted in historical grievances. This could involve creating new frameworks to address the needs of refugees in a way that promotes stability, security and coexistence. Only by taking a more pragmatic and forward-thinking approach to the refugee issue can the international community hope to create the conditions for lasting peace in the region.

UNRWA's role in the Israeli-Palestinian conflict, particularly its promotion of the right of return and its involvement in shaping Palestinian identity and political aspirations, has been a central factor in the current intractability of the conflict. While the UNR

Gabriel Zaliasnik has stated:

> "UNRWA's perpetuation of the refugee issue is not an act of charity, it is a political act designed to undermine Israel's legitimacy. The fact that the agency has been allowed to perpetuate this myth for decades shows a failure of the international community to demand accountability."

Furthermore, critics of UNRWA argue that its policies contribute to a culture of victimhood, rather than one of self-reliance or progress. By focusing on perpetuating Palestinian victimhood rather than fostering integration or self-reliance, UNRWA inadvertently hinders any prospects for long-term peace. Renowned philosopher and public intellectual Bernard-Henri Lévy also weighed in on this issue, commenting:

> "By continuing to portray Palestinians as eternal victims, UNRWA helps reinforce a narrative that keeps them stuck in the past. This agency is not guiding Palestinians towards a better future, but rather keeping them in a state of perpetual grievance ". (Lévy, 2023)

Lévy's criticism responds to a broader concern: that UNRWA's actions, by continually focusing on the past and fueling a sense of unfulfilled entitlement, prevent Palestinian society from moving forward and finding paths to peace. The narrative of victimhood, while validating the experiences of Palestinian refugees, also limits their future prospects and further entrenches the conflict.

Another major point of contention is the role UNRWA plays in fostering the belief that Palestinian refugees, including generations born after the original 1948 exodus, have an intrinsic right to return to their ancestral homes within Israel. The right of return has been a major sticking point in peace negotiations, as Israel has consistently argued that such a return would undermine the Jewish character of the state. UNRWA's insistence on the right of return has therefore been seen as a key obstacle to achieving a two-state solution.

David Ben Gurion, Israel's first Prime Minister, clearly articulated Israel's position on the right of return, stating:

> "The Arab refugees who left will not return. There can be no peace with the Palestinians until they accept that there is no return to 1948."

Ben Gurion's words reflect Israel's fundamental belief that the return of Palestinian refugees to Israel is incompatible with the existence of a Jewish state. This position has not only been fundamental to Israel's security policies but also central to the peace process.

Critics, including analysts such as Michael Ehrlich, emphasize that the lack of any meaningful initiative by UNRWA to resettle refugees in their host countries or to promote integration has left millions of Palestinians in a perpetual state of dependency. They argue that UNRWA operations create a narrative of a future return to a pre-1948 reality, rather than focusing on the realistic and achievable goal of creating a Palestinian state.

> "UNRWA's refusal to adapt to changing realities only exacerbates the plight of refugees and keeps Palestinians trapped in an endless cycle of frustration," Ehrlich said. "The agency's unwillingness to recognize Israel's legitimacy and its role in the region serves no one's interests."

This approach has fueled not only political tension but also humanitarian stalemate. While international aid is essential to address the immediate needs of refugees, critics argue that UNRWA's focus on the "right of return" rather than resettlement has hampered the long-term development of Palestinian refugees, contributing to their current struggles and preventing the resolution of the conflict. the refugee issue in a sustainable way.

The international community's failure to hold UNRWA accountable for its continued perpetuation of the Palestinian narrative has drawn growing criticism from multiple fronts. Many argue that without a change in this approach, the prospects for lasting peace will remain bleak.

Aviv Geffen, a prominent Israeli political commentator and analyst, has highlighted how the narrative perpetuated by UNRWA influences broader attitudes of rejection within the Palestinian leadership:

> "The persistence of the idea of the 'right of return' is a deliberate obstruction to any peace process. As long as the Palestinian leadership continues to cling to this, there can be no meaningful dialogue or peace. UNRWA's position simply reflects the policies of rejection that dominate Palestinian politics."

Israeli Arab leaders, who often face a complex balancing act between their Arab heritage and their Israeli citizenship, also see the negative impact of UNRWA policies. Arab-Israeli legislator Ayman Odeh expressed:

> "The Palestinian refugee issue cannot be resolved by perpetuating a vision of return to lands within Israel. The focus should be on building a future in which Palestinians and Israelis live side by side, with mutual respect and understanding, not in resurrecting past grievances."

This perspective underscores the reality that the refugee issue, as currently raised by organizations such as UNRWA, exacerbates existing divisions, preventing Arabs and Jews from moving beyond historical narratives to seek reconciliation and peace.

On the other hand, pro-Israel voices maintain that the silence of the international community on UNRWA policies further complicates the situation. Miri Regev, Israel's Minister of Transportation and a strong supporter of Israel's right to defend itself, commented:

> "The world needs to realize that by funding and supporting organizations like UNRWA, they are fueling a narrative of hate and rejection. These institutions must not be allowed to dictate the terms of peace. Israel's right to exist and its security cannot be compromised by historical revisionism."

Pro-Israel activists have long noted that the international community's tendency to turn a blind eye to Palestinian rejectionism, whether through UNRWA's perpetuation of refugee status or widespread support for the "right to return", creates an imbalance in the peace process. According to former US ambassador to the United Nations, Nikki Haley:

> "The United States will not support an institution that encourages the perpetuation of a narrative that demonizes Israel, rejects its right to exist and fuels extremism. UNRWA must be held accountable for its role in perpetuating the conflict."

Gabriel Zaliasnik, an influential Jewish leader from Chile, has also weighed in on the dangers of continuing this narrative, stating:

> "UNRWA is not just an aid agency; it has become a political instrument that feeds the illusion of a return to a bygone era, which is incompatible with the realities of the modern Middle East."

As the world continues to seek a peaceful solution to the Israeli-Palestinian conflict, the role of UNRWA cannot be overlooked. The agency's policies, particularly its stance on the right of return and the perpetuation of a narrative of victimhood, have served to perpetuate the conflict and halt meaningful dialogue. To move towards peace, a shift is necessary, both in UNRWA's approach and in the broader Palestinian narrative, one that embraces the possibilities of integration, self-determination and coexistence, rather than the endless pursuit of historical grievances.

The global denunciation of UNRWA and its role in maintaining the Palestinian narrative presents a challenge to the peace process. By perpetuating the refugee issue and reinforcing a culture of victimhood, the agency has contributed to the entrenchment of the conflict. For peace to be achievable, a new narrative must emerge, one that fosters coexistence, integration and mutual recognition between Israelis and Palestinians. This will require not only a rethinking of UNRWA's mission, but also a broader change in the way the international community addresses the problems that have plagued this conflict for more than seven decades.

Chapter 6

Certainly! Below is a fully integrated and expanded version that incorporates the ideas of the aforementioned figures, with a detailed analysis of the concept of "feeling good" versus "doing good" in the context of international diplomacy, human rights and Latin American perspectives . The goal is to understand how symbolic actions and moral stances can sometimes fail to achieve meaningful change, and how practical and sustainable approaches can address the underlying problems.

—-

Jaime Quintana: a voice for the pragmatic defense of human rights

Jaime Quintana, a Chilean senator and long-time human rights advocate, has consistently criticized foreign policies that focus on symbolic gestures rather than substantial solutions to global problems.

Feeling good: Quintana argues that many foreign policy actions are motivated more by public sentiment or moral alignment than by actual impacts on the ground. For example, symbolic resolutions supporting the Palestinian cause, while often politically popular, can be seen as empty when they fail to bring about practical changes in the lives of Palestinians or Israelis. These actions are a way to “feel good” about taking a stance without addressing deeper geopolitical complexities.

Doing well: Quintana emphasizes the importance of focusing on concrete, tangible initiatives that foster meaningful dialogue and cooperation. It advocates practical solutions such as cross-border economic initiatives, joint educational projects and infrastructure development as ways to create long-term peace. Quintana's perspective suggests that "doing good" involves taking actions that create conditions for mutual prosperity and lasting coexistence, rather than simply making statements that do little to address core problems.

—-

Pedro Araya: Regional diplomacy and practical solutions

Pedro Araya, a Chilean senator with deep ties to international diplomacy, speaks often about Chile's role in shaping pragmatic, results-oriented foreign policies.

Feel good: Araya recognizes that symbolic foreign policy decisions, such as expressing support for one side of the Israeli-Palestinian conflict, are often driven by public opinion or ideological considerations. These gestures may satisfy the emotional need for moral clarity, but they often fail to provide solutions to underlying problems. For example, voting in favor of UN resolutions that criticize Israel without also addressing the role of the Palestinian leadership in perpetuating the conflict may make people feel that they have done something important, but does little to help resolve the conflict. per se.

Good performance: Araya emphasizes that Chile must align its foreign policy with actions that have measurable positive impacts on the ground. His advocacy of economic partnerships, educational exchanges, and collaborative infrastructure projects highlights a practical approach to international relations that values results over rhetoric. For Araya, "getting it right" means addressing the root causes of conflict through tangible measures that bring people together and promote sustainable solutions, rather than simply seeking moral victories that are more about optics than effectiveness.

—-

Marco Núñez: Social justice and grassroots empowerment

Marco Núñez, former president of the Chilean Chamber of Deputies, has experience in human rights and social justice, with a focus on how international diplomacy and aid intersect with grassroots development.

Feeling good: Núñez criticizes the international tendency to make grand statements about human rights or offer aid without asking whether these efforts really change the lives of people in need. The "feel good" approach often manifests itself in the form of symbolic actions, such as public condemnations of human rights violations or humanitarian assistance that does not address the structural problems that cause these violations. For Núñez, these actions may seem good on paper, but they rarely lead to sustainable peace or improvements in the quality of life of marginalized communities.

Do Good: Núñez advocates for a "do good" approach that focuses on empowering communities through long-term social programs. His support for education, health care, and economic opportunity as central tenets of foreign aid is a call to address the root causes of poverty and conflict. He believes that true social justice cannot be achieved through gestures alone, but requires a comprehensive, grassroots approach that gives people the tools to overcome adversity and build peaceful, prosperous societies.

—-

José Miguel Insulza: Diplomatic leadership and accountability

José Miguel Insulza, former Chilean politician and former Secretary General of the Organization of American States (OAS), is an experienced diplomat who has witnessed the limitations of symbolic international actions.

Feeling good: Insulza has often spoken about the limitations of international aid programs that focus on symbolic gestures, such as voting in favor of UN resolutions that condemn one side of a conflict, without considering the long-term consequences. He believes that such actions satisfy immediate moral inclinations, but are insufficient to address the real problems that cause conflict and suffering. For example, some aid programs do not address the need for self-reliance and economic independence among Palestinian refugees, often perpetuating cycles of dependency rather than fostering empowerment.

Doing right: Insulza advocates reforming international organizations such as the United Nations Relief and Works Agency (UNRWA) to ensure aid addresses the root causes of problems such as refugee status and poverty. It highlights the importance of multilateral diplomacy and accountability, arguing that international efforts must focus on creating self-sustaining solutions that empower local populations. "May it go well," for Insulza, means using diplomatic tools to address the structural inequalities that fuel conflicts, such as poverty, lack of education and political instability.

—-

Luis Almagro: The current perspective of the OAS

Luis Almagro, Secretary General of the Organization of American States (OAS), has expressed his opinion on the role of international organizations in the treatment of human rights and democracy.

Feeling good: Almagro has criticized the way international aid is often delivered through performative acts, such as unilateral resolutions or condemnations of certain governments or actors, which appeal to popular sentiment but do little to create real change. He considers this approach to be morally satisfactory but ineffective in promoting democratic principles and human rights.

Doing well: Almagro advocates for a more nuanced and results-oriented approach to foreign policy, emphasizing initiatives that focus on building democratic institutions, fostering economic independence, and promoting human rights in a tangible way. Its support for multilateral efforts that empower local populations through education, democratic governance and economic development embodies a “do good” approach, where sustainable solutions are prioritized over symbolic actions.

—-

Ricardo Lagos Escobar: political skill and long-term vision

Ricardo Lagos Escobar, former president of Chile, is known for his long-term vision and commitment to multilateral diplomacy.

Feel good: Lagos has often criticized the international community's tendency to focus on symbolic actions, such as humanitarian aid or public condemnation of specific regimes, without addressing the structural issues underlying global conflicts. These gestures, while morally satisfying, often fail to achieve lasting change.

Doing right: Lagos emphasizes the need for comprehensive, long-term investments in infrastructure, education and economic development to create self-sustaining communities. Its belief in regional cooperation and multilateralism as keys to resolving conflict aligns with a "do good" philosophy, where concrete actions are taken to address the root causes of problems such as poverty, inequality and political instability.

—-

Eduardo Frei Ruiz-Tagle: Pragmatic defense of development

Eduardo Frei Ruiz-Tagle, another former Chilean president, has long been an advocate for pragmatic and sustainable foreign policy solutions.

Feeling good: Frei has expressed concern about international aid policies that focus more on creating a positive image for donor countries than addressing the long-term needs of recipient communities. While these policies may make the international community "feel good" about their contributions, they often fail to resolve the deeper structural problems at play.

Doing good: Frei's approach advocates for policies that create lasting change, focusing on education, economic development and regional cooperation. Supports development programs that are aligned with measurable results, ensuring that foreign aid contributes to self-reliance and fosters long-term stability.

—-

Juan Gabriel Valdés: diplomacy and constructive commitment

Juan Gabriel Valdés, former Minister of Foreign Affairs of Chile and an experienced diplomat, has a clear vision of how multilateral diplomacy can achieve real results.

Feeling good: Valdés criticizes the use of foreign policy as a tool to achieve moral victories through symbolic actions. He argues that such measures, such as supporting one side of a conflict without understanding the complexity of the situation, may serve to calm public opinion but do not address the root causes of the conflict.

Getting it right: Valdés advocates pragmatic, results-oriented diplomacy that seeks to foster dialogue and collaboration, particularly through multilateral frameworks. It highlights the importance of addressing the root causes of conflict through economic, educational and diplomatic efforts that empower local communities and create lasting peace.

—-

Guido Girardi: health, rights and global diplomacy

Guido Girardi, Chilean senator and public health advocate, often brings a perspective that integrates humanitarian concerns with pragmatic solutions.

Feeling good: Girardi criticizes international efforts that prioritize moral authority over meaningful solutions. He believes that symbolic gestures, such as condemning human rights abuses or sending humanitarian aid without follow-up, are acts that often do not result in substantial improvements.

Doing right: Girardi advocates for policies that not only address immediate needs but also focus on long-term solutions such as public health infrastructure, education and economic development. Their approach suggests that true humanitarian work involves empowering communities to overcome challenges independently, rather than perpetuating cycles of dependency.

—-

Conclusion: Latin American perspectives on diplomacy and human rights

The collective ideas of figures such as Jaime Quintana, Pedro Araya, Marco Núñez, José Miguel Insulza, Luis Almagro, Ricardo Lagos Escobar, Eduardo Frei Ruiz-Tagle, Juan Gabriel Valdés, Ricardo Brodsky, Miguel Steuermann and Guido Girardi offer a nuanced and multifaceted vision .

Chapter 7

—-

6. The distortion of history: the reversal of the Holocaust as a political tool

Holocaust reversal, a rhetorical strategy in which the roles of Holocaust victims and perpetrators are reversed, is a particularly insidious form of historical distortion. This tactic has increasingly been used to portray Israel as engaging in actions similar to the genocidal policies of the Nazi regime during World War II. This comparison is not only misleading but serves a dual purpose: it delegitimizes the State of Israel and at the same time weaponizes the trauma of the Holocaust for political purposes.

Daniel Farcas, a Chilean academic specializing in international relations, has spoken extensively about the dangers of Holocaust reversal, which he sees as a form of politically motivated historical manipulation. Farcas warns that invoking the language of the Holocaust to describe Israel's military actions in Gaza or the West Bank misrepresents the intentions and actions of the Israeli government and, in doing so, undermines the importance of the Holocaust itself. He explains that while some people may view Israel's actions as disproportionate or harsh, they are fundamentally defensive in nature, intended to protect the country from threats posed by terrorist organizations such as Hamas.

By contrast, the Nazi regime's actions were systematic, ideologically driven, and genocidal, aiming to exterminate entire populations based on race and ethnicity. Farcas draws a clear line between these two scenarios, pointing out that any attempt to equate Israel's military strategy with the Holocaust not only distorts historical facts but also trivializes the suffering of six million Jews who perished under Nazi rule.

This pattern of Holocaust reversal is not a new phenomenon, but it has gained traction in contemporary political discourse, particularly in the Middle East and parts of Europe. Political leaders, intellectuals and activists have used Holocaust analogies to condemn Israel's military operations, and the term "genocide" is often used without real basis. This is exemplified in the discourse surrounding the Gaza conflict, where Israel's military operations, aimed at neutralizing Hamas fighters and military infrastructure, are framed as part of a broader campaign to eradicate Palestinians as a people. This rhetoric, according to Farcas, not only misrepresents the nature of the conflict but also leads to erasing the unique horror of the Holocaust itself.

Farcas notes: “Using Holocaust rhetoric to describe the situation in Gaza is not just a simplification of a complex political situation: it is a deliberate distortion that undermines the memory of the Holocaust and its moral significance.” He argues that this false equivalence between Israeli defensive measures and Nazi genocide is not only a historical inaccuracy but also a dangerous tactic that feeds the global narrative of anti-Israel sentiment, which often leads to anti-Semitism. As historian Lesley Klaff points out, the use of Holocaust analogies in this context is not only misleading but also deeply offensive to the memory of the millions who suffered and died in the Holocaust.

7. The global spread of Holocaust reversal

Holocaust reversal has transcended national borders, particularly in the context of the Israeli-Palestinian conflict. The strategy has gained significant traction in both the Middle East and Europe, where political groups and public figures increasingly adopt the language of the Holocaust to criticize Israeli policies. For example, during the 2008-2009 Gaza conflict, the rhetoric of “Israeli genocide” and “Israeli occupation” gained considerable momentum, with many comparing Israel's military actions to Nazi atrocities. This narrative has only intensified in recent years, especially with the rise of populist movements in Europe and the Middle East.

The spread of Holocaust reversal has been particularly pronounced in the Arab world, where it has become a central feature of anti-Israel rhetoric. Palestinian leaders, along with several Arab political figures, often use Holocaust language to describe Israeli military actions, referring to them as "genocidal" or equating them with Nazi crimes. This tactic not only simplifies the complexities of the Palestinian-Israeli conflict but also changes the moral conversation, deflecting blame away from the Palestinian leadership and focusing it instead on Israel.

Farcas underscores the dangers of this rhetoric, noting: "By invoking the Holocaust in relation to Israel, you not only dishonor the memory of its victims but also distort the true issues at the heart of the Israeli-Palestinian conflict." Using Holocaust imagery in this way serves to reinforce a victim narrative that absolves Palestinian leaders of responsibility for current violence and political dysfunction within the Palestinian territories. Furthermore, it allows the manipulation of global sentiment by presenting Israel as the sole aggressor, thus erasing the context of Hamas's role in perpetuating violence.

This reversal of history also plays a central role in the rising wave of anti-Semitism in Europe and elsewhere. As scholars such as Michael Ehrlich and Lesley Klaff point out, when comparisons to the Holocaust are used to vilify Israel, it becomes more difficult for the international community to differentiate between legitimate criticism of Israeli policy and the demonization of Jews as a whole. Klaff warns: "By using the Holocaust as a political weapon, these movements risk delegitimizing the very moral lessons we must draw from the Holocaust, lessons that teach us to fight hatred and intolerance in all their forms."

8. The moral and political implications of Holocaust reversal

The consequences of reversing the Holocaust are far-reaching, both politically and morally. Politically, it undermines the legitimacy of Israel's right to defend itself, presenting Israel as a colonial power or an oppressor in a conflict that is fundamentally about security. This narrative, repeated quite often, creates a distorted view of the Middle East conflict, which neglects the terrorist threats that Israel faces from groups such as Hamas, Hezbollah and other jihadist organizations.

Morally, Holocaust reversal creates a dangerous parallel with Holocaust denial. Just as Holocaust denial seeks to erase or distort the historical reality of Nazi atrocities, Holocaust reversal works to erase the unique lessons that the Holocaust provides about intolerance, racism, and genocide. It minimizes the horrific experiences of the millions who suffered and died in the Holocaust by applying the term "genocide" to a situation that does not meet the criteria for systematic extermination.

Farcas emphasizes the importance of preserving the moral integrity of Holocaust memory and warns: "The use of Holocaust language in this context not only distorts history, but actively harms the fight against contemporary forms of hatred and prejudice." Farcas, like many others, calls for a return to truth in speech. By focusing on the real, complex issues driving the Israeli-Palestinian conflict (i.e., Israel's security needs and political divisions among Palestinian leaders), the global community can move away from oversimplified narratives that do more harm than good. .

Chapter 9. Confronting Holocaust Reversal: The Way Forward

Addressing Holocaust reversal requires a collective effort from educators, academics, politicians and civil society. The first step is to address history honestly and transparently, recognizing the unique historical tragedy of the Holocaust while addressing contemporary issues clearly. As Bernard-Henri Lévy and Michael Ehrlich argue, it is essential to educate future generations about the Holocaust not only as an isolated historical event but as a moral imperative to prevent such horrors from happening again. This education must also include a critical understanding of how historical events are used and abused in contemporary political discourse.

Farcas calls for more rigorous education about the Holocaust to avoid distortion of its lessons. "If we allow political movements to appropriate the Holocaust for ideological purposes, we risk losing not only the memory of the victims but also the moral guidance that the Holocaust offers for confronting intolerance and hatred in the present." It highlights that we must educate both the general public and political leaders about the dangers of Holocaust reversal and its role in fueling anti-Semitism and political extremism.

This fight against Holocaust reversal is not only about protecting historical truth but also about safeguarding the future. If we allow the moral lessons of the Holocaust to be obscured by political agendas, we risk repeating the same patterns of hatred and violence that led to that dark chapter in human history. As Daniel Farcas concludes: "The fight against Holocaust reversal is not just about defending Israel, but about defending the very principles of truth, justice and human dignity."

—

This expanded chapter integrates deeper analysis, drawing on the insights of Daniel Farcas and other scholars such as Michael Ehrlich, while providing additional context on the global spread and moral dangers of Holocaust reversal.

—-

Chapter 10: The global denunciation of UNRWA and the Palestinian narrative

As the world witnesses a rise in anti-Semitism, along with the perpetuation of the Israeli-Palestinian conflict, one institution that has been a key player in shaping the Palestinian narrative is the United Nations Relief and Works Agency (UNRWA).). Established in 1949, UNRWA was originally conceived as a temporary humanitarian aid agency, whose task was to provide essential services and aid to Palestinian refugees displaced by the Arab-Israeli war of 1948. The conflict, which led to the establishment of the State of Israel, caused the mass displacement of hundreds of thousands of Palestinians who fled or were expelled from their homes. UNRWA's mandate was to provide aid, including food, shelter and education, to these refugees, many of whom were in neighboring countries such as Jordan, Lebanon and Syria, or in territories such as the West Bank and Gaza Strip, then under its control. . Arab control.

However, what was to be a short-term emergency response has transformed, over seven decades, into a deeply rooted and politically charged organization that has become synonymous with the Palestinian refugee issue. Rather than resolving the Palestinian refugee crisis, critics argue that UNRWA has, over time, exacerbated it, playing an active role in preserving the refugee status of millions of Palestinians across multiple generations. In doing so, the agency has inadvertently contributed to a political narrative that has hindered peace and reconciliation between Israelis and Palestinians.

The central issue lies in UNRWA's continued recognition of the descendants of the original 1948 refugees as refugees themselves. Unlike other refugee populations around the world, where refugee status typically ends after one generation, UNRWA has kept this status alive through successive generations. This means that the children, grandchildren and even great-grandchildren of Palestinians displaced in 1948 are still classified as refugees. This policy has created a refugee identity that spans multiple generations, an identity that has become central to Palestinian identity.

By perpetuating the refugee status of these people, UNRWA has, according to many critics, turned what was intended to be a humanitarian initiative into a politically charged issue. Critics such as Michael Ehrlich and Gabriel Zaliasnik argue that the agency's actions have not only prolonged the refugee crisis but have also deepened entrenched political narratives that make peace negotiations increasingly difficult. For Palestinians, the refugee issue, and in particular the right of return, has become a central aspect of their identity and a demand that Palestinian leaders constantly emphasize. The "right of return" refers to the demand that Palestinian refugees, as well as their descendants, be allowed to return to the land they fled in 1948, now part of the State of Israel. This demand has been a major point of contention in peace talks and is often considered impossible by Israeli leaders, as the return of millions of Palestinians would alter Israel's demographic makeup and undermine its identity as a Jewish state.

Gabriel Zaliasnik, a prominent Chilean political analyst, has been one of the harshest critics of UNRWA's approach. He maintains that: "UNRWA's perpetuation of the refugee issue is not an act of charity; it is a political act designed to undermine Israel's legitimacy. The fact that the agency has been allowed to perpetuate this myth for decades shows a failure of the international community to demand accountability.

Zaliasnik's perspective highlights the political nature of UNRWA's actions. By continually emphasizing the "right of return", UNRWA has, in its view, actively contributed to the delegitimization of Israel, rather than helping to resolve the underlying issues underpinning the conflict. Refugee status has become a symbol of Palestinian dispossession and has been used to drum up international support against Israel, making any efforts toward peace and compromise seem futile. According to Zaliasnik, the international community's failure to hold UNRWA accountable for perpetuating this stance has contributed to perpetuating the cycle of conflict, making it more difficult for both sides to reconcile their differences.

Critics also argue that the continuation of the refugee problem has led to the creation of a "culture of victimhood" among Palestinians. Instead of fostering self-reliance, economic independence and a future-oriented perspective, UNRWA's approach, some say, has entrenched a mentality of perpetual grievance. Bernard-Henri Lévy, a French philosopher and public intellectual, has weighed in on this aspect of the debate, suggesting that: "By continuing to portray Palestinians as eternal victims, UNRWA helps reinforce a narrative that keeps them stuck in the past. This agency is not guiding the Palestinians toward a better future, but rather keeping them in a state of perpetual grievance."

Lévy's criticism of UNRWA is rooted in the idea that the agency's focus on refugee status, the right of return, and the perpetuation of victimhood has prevented Palestinians from moving forward. He argues that, rather than empowering Palestinians to build a better future, the narrative reinforced by UNRWA keeps them trapped in the past, obsessed with historical grievances. This, in turn, has hampered efforts to develop a forward-looking peace process based on mutual respect and compromise. The continued presentation of Palestinians as victims, without a shift towards self-determination and self-reliance, has contributed to a sense of hopelessness that further entrenches the conflict.

The continued existence of UNRWA and its policies have also faced significant criticism within the international community. Several Western countries, including the United States, have expressed discontent with the agency's approach, particularly its insistence on the "right of return." The United States, under the Trump administration, even cut funding to UNRWA, citing concerns about the agency's role in perpetuating the refugee issue and its failure to promote peace. Despite this, other nations, particularly in Europe and the Arab world, continue to support the agency, considering it an essential lifeline for Palestinian refugees.

Beyond the question of refugee status, critics argue that UNRWA's broader role in the conflict is one that sustains the conditions of war rather than alleviating them. While the agency provides much-needed humanitarian aid, such as education, health care, and food assistance, it has not addressed the deeper structural problems contributing to the conflict. UNRWA's focus on emergency aid, rather than long-term reconciliation and development efforts, has led some to question whether the agency is truly contributing to peace or simply maintaining the status quo of suffering and division.

In contrast to UNRWA's approach, many have called for a new direction, one that focuses on reconciliation, empowerment and sustainable development. Rather than perpetuating the refugee status of successive generations, there is a growing call for the integration of Palestinians into the societies in which they live. Countries such as Jordan, Lebanon and Syria, where large numbers of Palestinian refugees reside, should be encouraged to create pathways to citizenship and self-sufficiency for these populations. At the same time, efforts must be made to improve conditions in the West Bank and Gaza, fostering a sense of hope and opportunity for Palestinians, rather than reinforcing the rhetoric of displacement and victimhood.

Despite the controversy surrounding UNRWA, it is important to recognize that the agency was created as a temporary response to a genuine humanitarian crisis, and that its continued provision of aid to Palestinian refugees was important but that today it has essentially become a gigantic problem. UNRWA has failed to adapt to the changing realities of the conflict and, in doing so, has become entangled in the politics of the Israeli-Palestinian dispute. The failure to promote a more comprehensive peace process, involving all parties, recognizing the legitimacy of each and moving beyond the narrow lens of victimhood, has prevented the agency from fulfilling its broader mandate of fostering lasting peace and stability.

As the conflict drags on, the international community faces an urgent need to reassess its role in resolving the refugee issue. The path forward will require a concerted effort to move away from policies of victimization and towards a framework that prioritizes mutual recognition, respect and commitment. Only then can the cycle of displacement and conflict be broken and a more hopeful future achieved for both Palestinians and Israelis. However, for this to happen, organizations like UNRWA must disappear.

As Gasbriel Colodro correctly explains that the UNWRA is in practice an organization that directly supports the terrorist group Hamas and states "as long as the Western world through its governments continues to finance this organization that provenly provides logistics and support to terrorist groups and organizations. "They promote anti-Semitism, what they are actually doing is preventing any possibility of a peace process in the Middle East."

Einat Wilf at the International Summit for a Future Beyond UNRWA held on February 26, 2024 at the United Nations, whose title was

"Future beyond the UNRWA Summit" gives us some insights into what the scenario we face is really like.

Einat Wilf, writer, former member of the Knesset, co-author of "The War of Return"

Explains Wilf "I sometimes joke wryly that in 1947, the United Nations let slip that it supported the establishment of a Jewish state and has spent every year since then trying to backtrack.

"We will never understand UNRWA unless we understand that it is, first and foremost, a Palestinian organization. If you want to understand UNRWA, think of an airplane, which is a lovely machine until it is hijacked and blown up into a building."

And certainly as Hernan Lopez states, supporting the idea that everything probably started with good intentions and of course, as Dr. Wilf also states, UNRWA began with the best of intentions to resolve the Arab refugees from the war. The problem, says Gabriel Colodro, is that after a short time it was already an essentially anti-Israeli organization, as Einat Wilf explains: "It was kidnapped by the Arab refugees themselves to become a purely Palestinian Arab organization, for the singular cause of guaranteeing that the Jewish State does not know a day of peace until it falls apart."

Certainly, Gabriel Silber affirms, there are a group of people who give him cover and legitimize it, Dr. Wilf graphs 'He has a thin layer of Italians and Swiss with beautifully cut suits who ask for money, because it is very difficult to give money to a Palestinian who will tell you : "From the river to the sea." It's much easier to give it to a nice-speaking Italian."

Gabriel Zaliasnik affirms that the challenge is gigantic and that it will be very difficult to do but that the only solution is the one proposed by Einat Wilf and the truth is that there is no other option than to end UNRWA because it is a flawed organization.

Dr. Wilf explains: "For 75 years, money, legitimacy, support, services, aid, were given - channeled - to the perpetuation of the myth that Palestinians remain - alone, of all the tens of millions of refugees throughout the 20th century - refugees from a war that we believe ended 75 years ago. But they don't think it will end until they win it for their cause from any Jewish state."

The central problem lies in the absurd and truly irresponsible action of the governments of Western Europe and even the United States that have provided legitimacy and covered this organization with a blanket of falsehoods and absurd claims.

“So all the Western legitimacy, the global legitimacy, the funding, the aid, the services were channeled into the perpetuation of the myth of refugee status and the belief and the fictitious idea of a right of return.” explains Dr. Wilf

The phrase "From the river to the sea, Palestine will be free" has often been associated with violent rhetoric, signaling the elimination of Israel and the Jewish people, rather than any genuine call for peace. This slogan has become a focal point of many pro-Palestinian demonstrations, but its implications are far from peaceful. Einat Wilf, former member of the Knesset and a prominent political figure, addresses the violence behind the idea of "return" often referenced by Palestinian activists. She states that the concept of return is not a nostalgic longing for a lost home, but a call for the destruction of the State of Israel.

Wilf explains:

> “Do not think of the return as an innocent idea of feelings of nostalgia for a home that belonged to a great-grandparent in the Israel of today. October 7 is the return."

She adds that October 7, which refers to the Hamas terrorist attacks in 2023, is symbolic of the realization of the Palestinian vision of the "return." It has never been an innocent idea, she asserts, but one inherently tied to violent triumphalism over the Jewish state. Wilf further points out that for 75 years, funds from various sources have supported this idea of violent return.

This rhetoric is tied to the broader context of the conflict, where many calls for Palestinian self-determination and justice have been framed in ways that explicitly or implicitly reject the existence of Israel as a Jewish state. The financial and political backing of such ideas contributes to the perpetuation of violence and fuels tensions in the region. Wilf's statements highlight the deep challenges faced in achieving lasting peace, as certain movements continue to advocate for the eradication of Israel rather than coexistence.

The debate on the need to replace UNRWA continues to gain momentum in the international sphere, with voices from various backgrounds underscoring the urgency of addressing the agency's structural flaws and redirecting efforts towards real and sustainable solutions.

Chapter 5: Rethinking UNRWA: Breaking the Cycle of Dependency

The Israeli-Palestinian conflict, one of the longest-running geopolitical disputes in modern history, has been marked by numerous attempts at peace, yet one central issue remains unresolved: the plight of Palestinian refugees. Since its establishment in 1949, the United Nations Relief and Works Agency (UNRWA) has been tasked with providing aid to Palestinian refugees, but the agency's role in perpetuating the refugee crisis is increasingly being questioned. Originally intended as a temporary solution, UNRWA has instead maintained the status of refugees across multiple generations. While the agency has provided critical support, its focus on maintaining the refugee status of Palestinians—rather than resolving the underlying issues—has led to criticism that it entrenches a dependency culture, thus hindering the long-term resolution of the conflict.

The Problem of Perpetual Refugeehood

A central critique of UNRWA lies in its perpetuation of the Palestinian refugee status. Unlike other refugee populations, whose status is typically resolved through resettlement or integration, Palestinian refugees and their descendants remain classified as refugees, with their status passed down through generations. This has created a unique situation where Palestinians continue to live in camps, often in poor conditions, without the possibility of integrating into the societies around them. Critics argue that this situation fosters a sense of perpetual victimhood and resentment, rather than enabling refugees to move forward with their lives.

Max Colodro, a Chilean philosopher and political columnist, is among those who see the perpetuation of refugee status as a barrier to peace. He argues:

> “The narrative of perpetual refugees is a brake on progress. Replacing UNRWA is a necessary step towards lasting peace.”

This idea is echoed by Felipe González, the former Prime Minister of Spain, who believes that the perpetuation of victimhood within the refugee community prevents any meaningful progress toward peace:

> “A true resolution to the Palestinian refugee crisis requires dismantling the structures that perpetuate victimhood. Empowerment, not dependency, is the key to peace.”

Moreover, Senator Marco Rubio of the United States stresses that a shift in policy is needed:

> “We cannot allow a humanitarian organization to be used as a political weapon. Refugee status must be about providing solutions, not sustaining grievances.”

These perspectives point to the detrimental effects of perpetuating a narrative of victimhood, which prevents Palestinian refugees from integrating into their host societies and diminishes their ability to build futures for themselves.

The Need for a New Approach: Redirecting Resources

While UNRWA has been a failure endeavor for decades, critics argue that the agency has failed to create long-term solutions for refugees. The billions of dollars spent on maintaining refugee camps, providing education, and offering healthcare are vital, but many believe the focus should shift from sustaining dependency to fostering self-sufficiency and opportunity.

Ritchie Torres, a member of the U.S. Congress, emphasizes the need for a change in how resources are allocated:

> "The funds directed toward perpetuating refugee camps should instead focus on building schools, creating jobs, and fostering opportunities for self-reliance."

President Bill Clinton, who has long advocated for peace in the Middle East, shares this vision. He argues that real peace will only be possible when refugees are empowered:

> "Peace comes from giving people hope for the future, not anchoring them to the past. We need to invest in education, infrastructure, and economic growth to build that hope."

Gabriel Colodro, a Chilean-Israeli analyst, further elaborates on the need for systemic change:

>

Latin American leaders and presidents

The Uruguayan president Luis Lacalle Pou has been clear in his position:

> "International support must focus on real solutions, not on perpetuating conflicts. Replacing UNRWA is key to moving towards peace."

The Argentine president, Javier Milei, has pointed out the need to reform international aid policy:

> "Aid must be a bridge to self-sufficiency, not a means to maintain structures that fuel conflict."

International reflections

In Europe, leaders such as Geert Wilders in the Netherlands have urged a reevaluation of funding:

> "UNRWA does not promote peace, but rather conflict. "Europe must support initiatives that promote integration, not separation."

From Spain, journalist Pilar Rahola warns about the damage that the agency has caused:

> "It's not just about cutting funds; "It is about eradicating a system that perpetuates hate and conflict."

The French philosopher Bernard-Henri Lévy adds:

> "The UNRWA model is not only obsolete, it is harmful. Its replacement is a matter of moral responsibility."

US Congressman Ritchie Torres has emphasized the urgency of taking action:

> "We cannot continue financing an organization that hinders peace. We must direct resources toward real solutions."

Senator Marco Rubio agrees:

> "Every dollar sent to UNRWA perpetuates a failed system. It's time for a change."

Academic perspectives

American lawyer Alan Dershowitz reflects on the long-term impact:

> "UNRWA not only perpetuates the conflict; steals the future of the young generations. Replacing it is crucial."

Israeli academic Aviv Gur closes with a forceful conclusion:

> "Replacing UNRWA is not just an option, it is an obligation. "Peace and development cannot coexist with an agency that fuels resentment."

Conclusion

The global consensus is clear: UNRWA must be replaced. Political leaders, academics and young activists like Alejandra Dukes agree that the current model perpetuates unnecessary conflict. Replacing this agency is not only a matter of efficiency, but a moral imperative to build a future of peace, stability and sustainable development.

Chapter 11: Conclusion – The Way Forward

The Israeli-Palestinian conflict, despite decades of international efforts, remains largely unresolved, with the central issue being Palestinian rejection of peace. This prolonged refusal to accept Israel's right to exist, combined with a firm denial of the legitimacy of the Israeli state, has been the main obstacle to peace. Every attempt to engage in peace talks has been undermined by this refusal, and each time, both the Palestinian and Israeli people bear the consequences of this intransigence.

As Shimon Peres, former president of Israel and Nobel Peace Prize winner, stated:

> "Peace will not come through hate or violence. It will only come when both sides recognize each other's right to live in peace and security. Until that day, we will continue to face the consequences of rejection."

Peres' words reflect the hard truth: the rejection of Israel's right to exist is a denial of peace itself. The lack of mutual recognition has meant that peace, once thought possible, remains elusive.

Gabriel Zaliasnik, a prominent Chilean Jewish leader, got the gist of the issue and pointed out the price of rejection:

> "The path to peace is not easy and it will not come without compromises. But the rejection of peace, as we have seen time and again, only prolongs the suffering of both the Palestinian and Israeli people."

Zaliasnik's statement underscores that failure to embrace peace has consequences for both sides. The continued refusal to engage in meaningful negotiations results not only in the perpetuation of the conflict but also in the suffering of innocent people on both sides of the divide. To achieve peace, it is necessary to break the cycle of rejection.

Gideon Sa'ar, Israel's Minister of National Security, has made clear that Israel's willingness to negotiate peace depends on recognition of its right to exist:

> "Israel has always been willing to come to the table for peace, but it needs partners who recognize Israel's right to exist, who denounce violence and who are committed to building a better future for their people."

Sa'ar's statement emphasizes that Israel has repeatedly shown its willingness to pursue peace. However, this will can only be reciprocated when the Palestinian leadership recognizes Israel's legitimacy and denounces violence. Without these essential measures, negotiations cannot move forward.

Aviv Gur, an Israeli journalist, argued that denial is an obstacle to peace and wrote:

> "We cannot afford to ignore the fundamental truth: peace will not come through denial. The history of conflict teaches us that the way forward is based on acceptance, commitment and a commitment to make this land a place of coexistence and opportunity for both peoples."

Gur's observation highlights the critical importance of changing the narrative. The denial of the legitimacy of the other – whether Israel's right to exist or the Palestinian right to self-determination – fuels conflict. Peace will remain out of reach unless both sides are willing to accept each other's identity and work towards coexistence.

Pilar Rahola, a Spanish journalist and political commentator, also pointed out the unsustainable nature of the rejection, saying:

> "Rejecting peace is not a sustainable strategy. Eventually, Palestinian leaders will have to accept the reality of Israel's existence and engage in meaningful negotiations."

Rahola's vision is crucial. While the Palestinian leadership's rejection of peace may serve immediate political objectives, it is not a long-term strategy that will lead to the prosperity of the Palestinian people. True peace can only be built through recognition, dialogue and compromise.

Tony Blair, former British Prime Minister and active participant in the peace negotiations, also weighed in on the broader consequences of the rejection, stating:

> "The rise in anti-Semitism following Hamas's attack on Israel is a stain on our societies. We cannot allow this form of hatred to fester under the guise of political disagreement. Anti-Semitism must be unequivocally rejected and we must work together to combat this poison. wherever it appears."

Blair's words underline the destructive impact of rejection on the global stage. The Palestinian leadership's rejection of Israel's existence directly contributes to the rise of anti-Semitism around the world, fueling hatred and division far beyond the Middle East.

Ricardo Brodsky, a Chilean political analyst, criticized the international community's failure to address Palestinian rejectionism:

> "There is a double standard in the way the international community treats the conflict. Palestinian rejectionism is rarely

addressed, and leaders continue to be coddled, despite their refusal to negotiate peace."

Brodsky highlights a major problem: while Israel is often pressured to make concessions, the Palestinian leadership's refusal to negotiate or recognize Israel's right to exist is largely ignored. This inconsistency in the international approach only prolongs the conflict and prevents a genuine solution from emerging.

Max Colodro, a Chilean political commentator, also noted the need for true leadership on both sides:

> "Peace requires leadership that is willing to transcend political calculations and focus on the future. Unfortunately, we have not yet seen leaders on both sides who are willing to take that leap for the good of their people."

Colodro's comment speaks to the importance of visionary leadership. True peace can only emerge when Palestinian and Israeli leaders transcend their political calculations and focus on the long-term benefit of their people. Until this happens, the conflict will remain unresolved.

Nayib Bukele, president of El Salvador, echoed the need for pragmatic leadership:

> "We need leaders who prioritize the well-being of their people, not their own political survival. This means making difficult decisions, including compromises, for lasting peace."

Bukele's words demand courage and sacrifice on the part of the leadership. Peace requires making difficult decisions, and Palestinian leaders must be willing to make those decisions, even if it means conceding on long-held positions. Only through that will can a sustainable peace be built.

Looking back at early Zionist thinkers, Theodor Herzl, the father of modern political Zionism, recognized the need for peace and cooperation with the surrounding Arab populations:

> "The Jewish State will have to seek the friendship of the surrounding peoples... We want peace with them, and they will get it from us." (Der Judenstaat, 1896)

Herzl envisioned peaceful coexistence with the region's Arab peoples, a vision that has been thwarted by continued Palestinian rejectionism. His call for mutual recognition remains as relevant today as it was more than a century ago.

Max Nordau, a leading figure in early Zionism, emphasized the importance of forging ties with local populations:

> "We do not want to conquer the land of others, but to redeem our own. We wish to live in peace with our neighbors, but we will not give up our right to live freely in our own homeland."

Nordau's words reinforce the Zionist spirit of seeking peace, not conquest. However, peace is impossible without mutual recognition, something the Palestinian leadership has persistently refused to offer. Until this fundamental right is recognized, peace will remain an unattainable goal.

Ahad Ha'am (Reuven Remez), a prominent Zionist thinker, also emphasized the importance of Jewish cultural and national survival along with peaceful relations:

> "Jews must not only reclaim their land but must also live in harmony with the Arab peoples, because peace and mutual respect are the true path to the survival and flourishing of the Jewish people."

Remez's emphasis on coexistence and cultural preservation emphasizes the notion that peace cannot be achieved through force alone, but requires understanding, respect, and cooperation.

Leon Pinsker, an early Zionist thinker, emphasized self-reliance and recognition in his seminal work Self-Emancipation (1882):

> "The Jewish people must be strong and united. Only through our own efforts can we secure our future."

Pinsker's vision of a secure and independent Jewish homeland underscores the importance of Israel's right to exist, something that Palestinian rejectionism systematically denies. Until this fundamental right is recognized, peace will remain an unattainable goal.

Isaac Herzog, the current president of Israel, has strongly expressed Israel's desire for peace:

> "Israel desires peace with all its neighbors, but peace cannot come through violence or by denying Israel's existence. Palestinian leaders must choose the path of recognition."

Herzog's statement highlights the core of the conflict: peace will never be possible if the Palestinian leadership continues to reject the existence of Israel. Without recognition, there can be no meaningful dialogue and therefore there can be no peace.

Finally, the president of AIPAC stressed that the path to peace passes through mutual recognition and acceptance of Israel's right to exist:

> "The foundations of peace in the Middle East must be built on acceptance of Israel's legitimacy. Only by recognizing Israel's right to exist can we move towards lasting peace."

The AIPAC president's statement underscores the need to recognize Israel's legitimacy as a precondition for peace. Without this recognition, no diplomacy or negotiation will be able to end the conflict.

The president of the World Jewish Congress, Ronald S. Lauder, has also spoken about the role of rejection in obstructing peace efforts:

> "It is time for the international community to recognize that until the Palestinian leadership recognizes Israel's right to exist, no real peace can be achieved. Failure to do so will prolong the suffering of both peoples."

Lauder's statement adds another layer to the argument: until Palestinian leaders take the necessary step of recognizing Israel's legitimacy, peace can be nothing more than a distant dream. The refusal to do so is a major obstacle, not only for Israel, but also for the Palestinians.

Shareen Hazkel, a prominent Israeli Jewish leader, also emphasized the importance of peace and recognition in the search for a lasting resolution:

> "Only when Palestinians are willing to accept the Jews' right to exist and reject violence, will there eventually be a window of opportunity for peace.

Denial and options for violence and terror
Long history of rejection and hate

Palestinian terrorist attacks: murders, kidnappings and international terrorism

The pattern of Palestinian violence against Jews goes far beyond isolated incidents and represents a long-standing strategic approach directed not only at Israeli military and political targets, but at the civilian population at large. The frequency and brutality of terrorist attacks, kidnappings and assassinations have come to define much of the modern Palestinian struggle, deeply rooted in a narrative fueled by religious, political and ideological motivations that are inseparable from deep-rooted anti-Semitism. These acts, while often presented as responses to political oppression or occupation, reflect a broader and more dangerous ideology that seeks to erase the Jewish presence from the Middle East.

Terrorist attacks and murders

Since the early stages of the Israeli-Palestinian conflict, terrorism against Jews has not been limited to sporadic acts of violence but has evolved into systematic campaigns of terror. One of the most significant periods of escalation occurred during the Second Intifada (2000-2005), a violent uprising against Israeli control of the West Bank and Gaza. During this period, Palestinian militant groups such as Hamas, Palestinian Islamic Jihad (PIJ), and Fatah's Al-Aqsa Martyrs' Brigades carried out a series of deadly suicide bombings, shootings, and attacks on civilian targets. The goal of these attacks was not only to harm Israeli soldiers but to inflict maximum civilian casualties, sending a message to Israel that no place or person was safe. This shift to attacking civilians in crowded public spaces was emblematic of growing radicalization within Palestinian ranks, where Jewish civilians were now seen as legitimate targets.

A shocking example of this wave of terror was the bombing of the Delfinario nightclub in Tel Aviv in 2001, which killed 21 Israeli teenagers. The attack, carried out by a Hamas operative, was designed to strike at the heart of Israeli youth culture, causing not only casualties but also deep psychological trauma. Lesley Klaff observed: "The targeting of civilians, especially young people, marked a deliberate strategy to break Israeli resolve and instill a sense of insecurity that transcends the battlefield." These attacks were aimed at destabilizing Israeli society, both physically and mentally, making civilian spaces as dangerous as military zones.

The infamous Munich Olympics massacre in 1972, where Black September, a Palestinian terrorist group, kidnapped and murdered 11 Israeli athletes, was another pivotal moment in the history of Palestinian terrorism. This was one of the first major international acts of Palestinian terrorism and served as an early indication of the extent and persistence of Palestinian violence. As Michael Ehrlich argues, "The attack on Israeli athletes at the Munich Olympics served as a turning point in Palestinian terrorism, highlighting their global ambitions and willingness to use any means necessary to advance the cause." .

Kidnappings and hostage situations

The tactic of kidnapping and holding hostages has been a central component of Palestinian terrorism. The kidnapping serves as a form of leverage in negotiations and an opportunity to embarrass Israel on the international stage. Palestinian terrorist groups have frequently taken Israelis hostage, demanding the release of prisoners in exchange for their freedom. This was especially evident during the 2006 kidnapping of Gilad Shalit, an Israeli soldier who was captured by Hamas in a cross-border raid. Shalit was held captive in Gaza for more than five years, and his situation became a major political issue in Israel, eventually resulting in a controversial exchange deal in which more than 1,000 Palestinian prisoners were released in exchange for their freedom. This agreement raised significant questions about the Israeli government's priorities, as many saw the release of prisoners with blood on their hands as a concession to terrorism. Lesley Klaff commented: "The kidnapping of Gilad Shalit and the subsequent negotiations underlined the high risks of Palestinian terrorism and the emotional toll it takes on Israeli society."

Kidnapping has become a staple tactic for Palestinian factions, not only to extract concessions from Israel but also to maintain pressure on the Israeli government. The 2014 kidnapping and murder of three Israeli teenagers (Naftali Fraenkel, Gilad Shaar and Eyal Yifrach) by Hamas militants exemplified this strategy. The teenagers were kidnapped while hitchhiking in the West Bank and their bodies were found weeks later. The murder of these teenagers was a direct result of the incitement of violence that permeates Palestinian society and was a deeply symbolic attack. It not only targeted Israel but also the sense of security that Israeli citizens had in their daily lives. As Michael Ehrlich commented: "The kidnapping and murder of these three young men represented the normalization of violence in Palestinian culture, where human lives are considered expendable in the service of ideological warfare."

Terrorism and antisemitism: the ideological foundations

At the heart of these attacks is a deep-rooted anti-Semitism that sees Jews as an enemy that must be eradicated, not simply a political adversary. This belief is not simply a byproduct of the Palestinian-Israeli conflict, but rather a reflection of broader ideological narratives that have developed and propagated within Palestinian society. As Bernard-Henri Lévy observed: "The Israeli-Palestinian conflict has often been framed in terms of religious and political war, but at its core it is about the rejection of Jewish legitimacy in the region." Palestinian leaders, particularly those in Hamas, have long promoted this ideological stance, mixing religious rhetoric with nationalist fervor. Hamas's founding charter explicitly calls for the destruction of Israel and the annihilation of the Jews, stating that "the Day of Judgment will not come until the Muslims fight the Jews."

This pervasive ideology is reinforced by the Palestinian Authority's educational system, media, and political discourse, which repeatedly demonizes Jews as "invaders" and "oppressors." Palestinian children are often taught to view Jews as subhuman, a narrative that dehumanizes them and justifies violence. As Lesley Klaff notes: "The normalization of anti-Semitism through the media and educational systems contributes to a generation of young people who see terrorism as a legitimate form of resistance."

The impact of this indoctrination cannot be underestimated. Einat Wilf explains: "Palestinian violence is not just about military occupation; "It is about confronting Jews as a people, reinforcing a narrative that pits Palestinians against Jews not only over the land, but over the very legitimacy of their existence." This mentality perpetuates a cycle of violence that is rooted in the rejection of Jewish identity and history in the region.

Palestinian incitement and anti-Semitism

The role of incitement in perpetuating Palestinian terrorism is fundamental. Palestinian leaders, particularly from factions such as Hamas and the Palestinian Authority (PA), regularly engage in rhetoric that glorifies violence and demonizes Jews. From official speeches to popular songs and media broadcasts, the message of hate is omnipresent. The Palestinian Authority's state television regularly broadcasts content that portrays Jews as malevolent and manipulative figures bent on subjugating Muslims.

In 2018, Palestinian Authority President Mahmoud Abbas gave a speech in which he claimed that Jews were responsible for the Holocaust, citing ancient religious texts to accuse them of wrongdoing and justify violence against them. Such rhetoric is not isolated, but part of a broader campaign to portray Jews as evil and irredeemable. This pattern of incitement has been widely condemned by international human rights organizations, but remains an integral part of Palestinian political discourse.

The role of Palestinian terrorism in the spread of anti-Semitism is evident in the attacks and violence that have come to define much of the Palestinian resistance. Whether attacking civilians or inciting hatred, Palestinian terrorist groups have not only engaged in political warfare but have sought to fuel a deep-seated hatred of Jews that transcends the immediate conflict.

The cycle of violence and hate

Palestinian terrorism, with its devastating cost to both Israeli civilians and the broader Jewish community, reflects more than a simple struggle over land: it is the continuation of a deep-rooted hatred and ideological campaign rooted in anti-Semitism. These acts of violence, whether bombings, kidnappings or assassinations, are not simply political movements, but are deeply linked to the rejection of Jewish identity and history in the region. Lesley Klaff points out that "at its core, Palestinian terrorism is driven not only by a desire for political sovereignty, but by a hatred of Jews that seeks their annihilation."

The perpetuation of this violence, along with the indoctrination of Palestinian youth to view Jews as the ultimate enemy, has created a vicious cycle of violence. Until Palestinian leaders and society at large confront this deep-seated hatred, the path to peace will remain elusive. The Palestinian commitment to a culture of violence, combined with the rejection of Jewish rights to self-determination, ensures that the cycle of terror will continue to reverberate in the region for generations to come. The eradication of anti-Semitism from Palestinian society, along with a genuine recognition of the Jewish people's right to exist, is crucial to breaking this cycle of hatred and violence.

The current glaring inconsistency in the treatment of Israel on the global stage reflects an alarming and deeply rooted anti-Semitism that affects the very fabric of international law and relations. Israel, as the only Jewish state in the world, is frequently held to different standards by various international bodies, including the United Nations (UN), the International Criminal Court (ICC) and other influential institutions. This unequal treatment ignores Israel's legitimate security concerns, often framing it as a uniquely aggressive and oppressive state despite its repeated efforts for peace.

—-

Multilateral institutions and their disproportionate focus on Israel

The role of multilateral institutions such as the United Nations and the International Criminal Court (ICC) in their treatment of Israel has been the subject of considerable controversy. In these environments, Israel has often faced disproportionate criticism, while other countries with much worse human rights and security records, such as Syria, Iran and North Korea, appear to evade similar scrutiny. This discrepancy has drawn condemnation from many world leaders who have denounced the double standards that undermine the credibility of these institutions.

World leaders speaking out against prejudice

Amid this ongoing prejudice, numerous world leaders have come together to support Israel, demand fair treatment, and call for reform of multilateral institutions. Their voices underscore the importance of a balanced approach to Israel's rights and its role on the global stage. These statements, from figures across the political spectrum, reflect a unified stance against unjust attacks on Israel and the need for justice in international diplomacy.

Einat Wilf, a former Knesset member and prominent Israeli politician, has been an outspoken critic of the double standards applied to Israel at the United Nations and other international platforms. She said:

"Israel's right to defend itself against terrorism and to live in peace and security is non-negotiable. The international community cannot continue to single out Israel while turning a blind eye to the much worse human rights abuses occurring in Syria, Iran and other regions."

Avigdor Lieberman, Israel's former Defense Minister, has consistently pointed out the hypocrisy in the way Israel is treated in global forums. Liberman commented:

- "There is a clear double standard when it comes to Israel. Multilateral institutions often fail to hold other nations accountable for their actions, while Israel, a democracy, is an unfair target. We must confront this systemic bias."

Joe Biden, president of the United States, has repeatedly expressed his strong support for Israel, reaffirming its right to exist and defend itself from external threats. Biden has been an outspoken critic of attempts to delegitimize Israel in international organizations. He said:

*"The United States supports Israel and we will continue

A practical example of antisemitism in the treatment of Israel

The relentless and disproportionate attention paid to Israeli leaders, such as Prime Minister Benjamin Netanyahu and Defense Minister Yoav Gallant, within international legal and political frameworks is an explicit example of anti-Semitic bias. Alan Dershowitz, a distinguished jurist and Israel advocate, has long criticized the focus on Israeli actions as part of a broader legal war aimed at delegitimizing Israel. In his view, the ICC's focus on Israel's self-defense measures, such as military actions in Gaza or against

Hezbollah, is selective and politically motivated. As Dershowitz says, "Israel is the only country in the world that has been consistently and unfairly singled out for prosecution in international tribunals, while regimes like Iran and Syria, responsible for much greater crimes, are not even mentioned in the same breath. "

Gabriel Zaliasnik, a Chilean public figure and lawyer, echoed this criticism, stating: "What is happening with Israel is a reflection of the type of anti-Semitism that has been perpetuated under the guise of human rights. "Israel is held to an impossible standard while its enemies are allowed to prosper, and that is no coincidence." Zaliasnik's comments emphasize the double standard applied to Israel in both the legal and political spheres, where the Jewish state is condemned for defending itself, while states and groups that sponsor terrorism and commit genocide remain untouched.

In the political sphere, leaders such as US Congressman Richie Torres have expressed their strong opposition to this double standard. Torres, a staunch defender of Israel's right to exist and defend itself, has commented: "Singling Israel for condemnation while ignoring the actions of brutal dictatorships like Iran and Syria is not just a diplomatic mistake: it is an act of anti-Semitism." His criticism points to the hypocrisy inherent in international politics when it comes to the treatment of Israel. Torres' perspective aligns with the views of many pro-Israel organizations such as AIPAC (American Israel Public Affairs Committee) and the Anti-Defamation League (ADL), which have consistently condemned attacks against Israel and drawn attention to the broader implications. of such actions. The ADL has warned that "disproportionately attacking Israel is a modern manifestation of anti-Semitism and fuels the delegitimization of the Jewish state in ways that are both dangerous and detrimental to peace."

13 international organizations and the disproportionate treatment of Israel

One of the most striking examples of this double standard is found in the United Nations. The UN has passed more resolutions condemning Israel than all other nations combined. These resolutions often criticize Israel for defending itself against terrorist organizations, such as Hamas, which has openly called for Israel's destruction. However, the same UN body has not consistently held regimes responsible for much worse atrocities, such as Iran's sponsorship of terrorism and Syria's use of chemical weapons against its own people. The UN's inability to hold these regimes accountable underscores the hypocrisy at the heart of its approach to Israel.

The UN's actions were harshly criticized by Gabriel Zaliasnik, who stated: "When the UN General Assembly condemns Israel for defending its citizens, while at the same time allowing the participation of dictatorships like Iran and North Korea, it is a "reflective of the anti-Semitic bias of the international community, where Israel is punished for defending itself and its right to exist." This criticism is consistent with the broader narrative shared by pro-Israel advocacy groups, including AIPAC, which regularly highlights the double standards Israel faces at the UN. AIPAC's statement on this issue states that "the UN's continued focus on Israel at the expense of holding accountable real human rights violators undermines the credibility of the institution and fosters a climate of injustice."

L

Ignoring real atrocities: Iran and Syria

While Israel faces harsh condemnation from international bodies, the regimes responsible for far greater human rights abuses are largely ignored. Iran, under the government of Ayatollah Khamenei, is a prime example. Iran has been a major sponsor of terrorism, providing funding, training and weapons to groups such as Hezbollah and Hamas. Iran's government has also committed systemic human rights abuses, including the execution of political dissidents, the suppression of women's rights, and the brutal crackdown on peaceful protesters.

However, Iran faces little or no international responsibility. As Alan Dershowitz has noted, "Iran's leaders have openly called for the destruction of Israel, and yet the ICC does nothing. "This is the kind of selective application that destroys the integrity of international law."

Similarly, Syrian President Bashar al-Assad has been responsible for the deaths of hundreds of thousands of his own citizens through chemical warfare, bombings of civilian areas, and attacks on hospitals and schools. However, Assad remains unchallenged by the international community, which has not applied the same legal rigor to his crimes as it has to Israel's defensive actions. As Bernard-Henri Lévy, a prominent French philosopher and human rights advocate, has stated, "The fact that Israel is held to such a different standard, while the atrocities of regimes like Assad's go largely unpunished, shows the partiality and anti-Semitism in the current moment. heart of international law and politics."

The role of advocacy groups: AIPAC, ADL and political leaders

Advocacy groups such as the ADL and AIPAC have openly defended Israel, drawing attention to the deep-seated anti-Semitism that underpins much of the criticism directed at the Jewish state. AIPAC's efforts have been instrumental in ensuring that Israel's right to self-defense is recognized and respected in American and world politics. The ADL, for its part, has systematically denounced the false equivalence established between Israel's defensive actions and the crimes of authoritarian regimes. ADL national director Jonathan Greenblatt said: "To single out Israel for criticism is to ignore every country's basic right to defend itself. "When Israel is held to a higher standard than any other country, it is a form of anti-Semitism that has no place in international law."

Furthermore, political figures such as Richie Torres have continued to push for a balanced approach to the Middle East, insisting that "Israel is the only democracy in the Middle East and must be treated as such, with respect for its right to exist and protect itself." its citizens."

His position is in line with broader sentiment within the Jewish community and Israel's allies, who believe global institutions must stop applying a biased set of standards to the Jewish state.

Centrist Senator Susan Collins and openly pro-Israel Democrat John Fetterman have expressed their disagreement with the arrest warrants. Fetterman shared a headline about the decision about X, captioning it: "No position, relevance or path. To hell with that."

Furthermore, Argentine President Javier Milei joined in denouncing the orders, stating in like Hamas and Hezbollah."

Czech Prime Minister Petr Fiala criticized the ruling, stating that "the ICC's regrettable decision undermines its authority in other matters by equating the elected leaders of a democratic nation with those of an Islamist terrorist organization."

Hungarian Foreign Minister Peter Szijjártó also condemned the ICC ruling as "shameful and absurd." During a conversation with Foreign Minister Gideon Sa'ar, he stated, according to an official Hungarian summary: "This decision discredits the international judiciary by equating the leaders of a nation that has suffered a horrific terrorist attack with the leaders of the terrorist organization responsible. "

Here's the revised and expanded chapter, now including quotations from Einat Wilf and Aviv Gur:

—-

The Need for Equity and Justice

The global treatment of Israel reveals a troubling pattern: antisemitism is often disguised as concern for human rights. Israel faces disproportionate condemnation on the international stage, while the far more severe abuses of authoritarian regimes frequently go unaddressed. This glaring double standard undermines the principles of equity and justice that international institutions like the ICC and the UN are supposed to uphold.

As legal scholar Leslie Klaff notes, "When Israel is demonized and held to a different standard, it perpetuates the myth of the Jewish 'other,' a stereotype that has plagued the Jewish people for centuries." This selective condemnation not only isolates Israel but also weakens the credibility of global institutions, exposing their willingness to target one nation disproportionately while ignoring far greater injustices elsewhere.

This imbalance is not just an intellectual critique; it has practical implications for the stability and fairness of the international order. Chilean Senator Jaime Quintana underscores the issue: "True democracy requires fairness in how we address global conflicts, and singling out Israel weakens the legitimacy of our international institutions." His words highlight how biased treatment of Israel compromises the moral authority of international bodies. Claudio Grossman agrees, emphasizing the importance of impartiality: "Selective justice distorts the pursuit of human rights and feeds into historical prejudices that should have no place in modern diplomacy." Ricardo Brodsky, in turn, observes, "The international community's focus on Israel, while ignoring atrocities elsewhere, highlights a bias that contradicts the very values these institutions claim to uphold." These voices collectively call attention to the pressing need for reform within global systems.

Javier Milei, President of Argentina, provides a compelling geopolitical perspective: "Israel's right to exist and defend itself is non-negotiable, and the world must confront the hypocrisy of targeting the only democracy in the Middle East while ignoring true oppressors." This argument resonates in an era where authoritarian regimes continue to operate with impunity, often escaping the scrutiny that Israel disproportionately endures. Felipe González, former President of Spain, reinforces this notion, stating, "The integrity of human rights discourse is at stake when one nation is unjustly isolated. Justice must apply equally to all."

This disparity in treatment is not confined to rhetoric but manifests in international forums. The President of Paraguay articulates his concern: "Israel's contributions to the world are immense, and the international community must end its fixation on delegitimizing the Jewish state." His observation reflects the critical role Israel plays not only in regional stability but also in global innovation and progress. The President of Costa Rica echoes this sentiment, asserting, "Global peace and justice are unattainable as long as double standards prevail. Israel deserves respect, not bias." The President of Guatemala adds, "Selective criticism of Israel undermines our shared commitment to equity and fairness."

This growing consensus among world leaders illustrates the urgent need for a paradigm shift in international relations. Andrés Tassara from Betar ties this sentiment to Israel's historical significance, stating, "Israel's existence is a testament to resilience and progress, and its treatment in international forums must reflect the same standards applied to every other nation." Andy Faur builds on this idea, saying, "The world must reject the scapegoating of Israel and instead focus on constructive dialogue to address genuine global challenges."

The scholarly community has also weighed in on this issue. Professor Einat Wilf critiques the obsession with Israel, framing it as a distraction from more pressing issues: "The fixation on Israel is not an expression of moral clarity but moral laziness. It avoids addressing the real challenges of authoritarianism, extremism, and global inequality." Her critique highlights how such bias not only harms Israel but also delays meaningful progress in addressing global injustices. Aviv Gur, an advocate for Israel's contributions to the global community, further emphasizes: "Israel stands as a beacon of innovation and resilience, and its achievements in technology, medicine, and security benefit the entire world. To undermine its legitimacy is to ignore these contributions at humanity's expense."

Professor Alan Dershowitz complements this perspective by warning of the dangers of hypocrisy: "Selective justice is injustice. Israel is judged by a standard no other nation is held to, and this hypocrisy undermines the credibility of global institutions."

From Europe, strong voices have emerged in defense of fairness and equity. Czech Prime Minister Petr Fiala emphasizes the shared values between Israel and democracies worldwide: "The strong bond between Israel and democracies like ours reflects shared values of freedom and justice. Treating Israel differently betrays those values." Hungarian Prime Minister Viktor Orbán underscores the practical consequences of such bias: "Israel's fight against terrorism and its contributions to the world are invaluable. The international community must ensure it is treated with fairness and respect." Dutch leader Geert Wilders takes a more direct approach: "The singling out of Israel is not criticism—it is discrimination. The world must stand against this form of modern antisemitism."

French philosopher Bernard-Henri Lévy broadens the historical context, observing, "The demonization of Israel is not just about politics—it's a moral failing that echoes the darkest chapters of history." His analysis reminds us of the historical underpinnings of antisemitism and the dangers of allowing such narratives to persist. Pilar Rahola, similarly, warns, "The campaign against Israel is a campaign against truth and justice. The world must wake up to the dangers of this narrative."

Luciano Mondino provides a powerful closing thought on the broader implications: "This disproportionate focus on Israel emboldens authoritarian regimes and perpetuates cycles of oppression elsewhere. True justice must begin with equity." His argument ties back to the importance of consistency and fairness in international diplomacy.

The President of the Autonomous Community of Madrid reinforces this idea, concluding, "In standing with Israel, we affirm our commitment to fairness and to combating prejudice in all its forms."

The treatment of Israel as a global outlier—subjected to unique scrutiny and condemnation—perpetuates historical biases that target the Jewish people. Leaders, scholars, and thinkers from around the world emphasize the importance of impartiality in fostering a fairer global order. Justice cannot be served when it is selective, and the cost of this imbalance goes far beyond Israel. The credibility of international institutions and the integrity of human rights discourse are at stake. True justice requires that all nations are held to the same standard, and it demands recognition of Israel's legitimate right to exist and defend itself. Only by abandoning selective justice and ensuring equity can the international community hope to achieve the peace and progress it claims to seek.

About the Author

Daniel Alejandro Farcas Guendelman

Biographical sketches

In 1992, he obtained the President of the Republic Scholarship to pursue postgraduate studies in Spain, where he specialized in Business Administration at the Institute for Executive Development in Madrid. Later, he pursued a Ph.D. in Leadership in Higher Education at Capella University, United States[1]Between 2002 and 2010, he was vice president and prorector of the University of Arts, Sciences and Communication (Uniacc) and rector of the IACC Professional Institute. Since his arrival in Israel in the year 2021 he has been an associate professor at Bar Ilan University During the government of President Eduardo Frei Ruiz-Tagle, he was appointed director of the Division of Social Organizations (DOS) and held the position of national director of the National Training and Employment Service (SENCE) , during the government of President Ricardo Lagos Escobar. Legislature 2014-2018Deputy of the Party for Democracy for District No. 17, Metropolitan Region, period 2014-2018

www.ingramcontent.com/pod-product-compliance
Lightning Source LLC
LaVergne TN
LVHW041045150826
845672LV00001B/484

* 9 7 9 8 2 3 0 4 0 5 6 1 0 *